Fifty Years by the Bay

The San Francisco Giants 1958-2007

by
Chuck Nan

Bloomington, IN 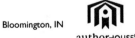 Milton Keynes, UK

authorHOUSE®

AuthorHouse™
1663 Liberty Drive, Suite 200
Bloomington, IN 47403
www.authorhouse.com
Phone: 1-800-839-8640

AuthorHouse™ UK Ltd.
500 Avebury Boulevard
Central Milton Keynes, MK9 2BE
www.authorhouse.co.uk
Phone: 08001974150

First published by AuthorHouse 11/1/2006

ISBN: 1-4259-6573-3 (sc)

Library of Congress Control Number: 2006908636

Copyright Number 2004: TXu1-176-500

Printed in the United States of America
Bloomington, Indiana

This book is printed on acid-free paper.

Dedication & Acknowledgements

This book is dedicated to many special people in my life.

Louis and Marge Nan

My wonderful parents. Thank you for giving me life, love and security. Thank you for the positive guidance and everlasting support. Thank you for teaching me to dream about the person I could become.

Holly Nan

My loving wife. Thank you for encouraging me to discover the artist within. Thank you for allowing me to be who I am. Thank you for believing in me.

Lily and Ellie Nan

My trusted special assistants. They do not make coffee, file documents, or take messages, but these girls sure are the best four-legged listeners I know.

I also acknowledge these other folks that have had a positive impact on my career and / or in the creation of this book.

Kevin Chroust

My primary proofreader and editor. Without him, I would be sunk. Kevin is a young an energetic professional with a bright future as a journalist.

Ed Attanasio

My secondary proofreader and editor. Not only is Ed very thorough and professional in what he does, but he is one of the most loyal baseball fans I have ever met.

Mike "Moose" Maxwell

Mike gave me my start in coaching at Giants' Youth Camp, one day out of the blue, with just a telephone call.

Tod Fierner

My trusted friend and photographer helped me out when I needed a snapshot. He really captures the true essence in athletics.

Special Thank You and Acknowledgement

"The Doc"

In the course of one's life, you are blessed with meeting people that have a profound impact on your life. For me, it was one special person, my close friend, Dr. Robert A. Jeffrey, Jr., M.D.

I was always a stat head since my early days of following sports. In 1975, I met the doctor and assisted him with game statistics at my high school. Soon "Doc" introduced me to the vast world of in-depth sports statistic tracking, documentation and analysis. He taught me that each game was an individual masterpiece that would endure in the archives forever.

In the late-1960s, Bob volunteered to be the Sports Information Director at St. Ignatius College Preparatory in San Francisco. From that point, he was tracking game plays and producing statistics in the way that you see many leagues (NBA, NFL, etc.) and media giants (ESPN, etc.) provide today on the Internet, some 35 years ago. The most amazing thing? **He did it all by hand!** He had only the help of a small group of assistants. These were usually students, grade school children or sons and daughters of coaches. Finally, he broke down and purchased an electric typewriter that he used at football games starting in the mid-1970s.

He has always been an inspiration to me and I strive to be as professional and precise in my approach to every project in my life.

A dedicated family man, compassionate physician and devout Christian man, we lost him way too early. The memory of his vision, dedication and loyalty endures.

Contents

Forward

There will be those who say this is a trivia book. There will be those that say this is a history book. There may be some who look at this work and say that it resembles an almanac. Still, there will be those who say that it is a story book, based upon fact. They are *all* correct.

In writing this book, I wanted to create a lasting work that would appeal to all fans, all readers. I wanted to appeal to the dedicated fan and the casual fan. I wanted to appeal to stat heads and folks who do not put any weight at all in the numbers of baseball. I wanted to appeal to *everyone* who picked it up.

In short, I wanted to create a composition that would tell the *entire* story of the Giants' fifty fabulous years in San Francisco.

Those who know me know that I am a very detail oriented person. I like to accumulate the whole story and every bit of fact or data available. Only then do I begin the process of analyzing, interpreting and evaluating.

I think it would be unfair to ignore or eliminate any aspect of the Giants' existence, even so minute or inconsequential, as some people may feel. Some of the story is told via statistics or numbers. Some of the story is told via narration. Some of the story is told via comparison-contrast. Some of the story is told via first-hand account. Some of the story is told via combinations of tools. The important thing is that the whole story is told.

Over fifty years, there has been a lifetime of stories. I seek to recount each of them, weave them together, and create a true snapshot of this place in time.

CGN

Introduction

When you have 50 years of something, it can describe as an "institution." This applies to just about anything or anyone. With this, you are bound to have many memories, a lifetime full of them. Memories are not always of the joys, successes, bright spots or good times. There is also going to be pain. For without the pain, then the success has no true meaning, perspective or substance. I refer to the feeling deep down in the soul. I am not going to be existential with this work, at all. But overall, my key point of focus is the celebration of something that has endured for a significant period of time.

When the San Francisco Giants take the field in April, 2007, it will be their 50th season in the City by the Bay. The Giants' franchise migrated west to open play in San Francisco for the 1958 season. The dawn of a new era in Major League Baseball was born; baseball was now bi-coastal and national. Since then, there have been many, many moments of note in team history. There have also been countless memorable players donning the orange and black uniform. There have been unforgettable performances, superb seasons and Hall-of-Fame careers. In some instances, the record book has been rewritten by some of these men and new standards set.

The Giants had a storied history from their 70-plus years in Gotham. Upon their arrival here, they continued that glory without skipping a beat. The Giants have had an endless stretch of exceptional, noteworthy and intriguing players. The franchise has been blessed with athletes who have punctuated the game with their own mark. Some have been recognized as stars that shaped the game itself.

I will never forget the excitement and thrill of going to my first game, about 1970 or so. It sounds corny, but it was one of those rights of passage that is talked about so much. True to form, I shared the memorable moment with my father and grandfather. How about the team on the field? The Giants had Mays, McCovey, Marichal and Perry. Throw in Bobby Bonds, Tito Fuentes, and Dick Dietz. Wow! Steve Carlton was pitching for the St. Louis Cardinals. How much better can it get? I cannot forget the hot dogs with sauerkraut, salted peanuts and cotton candy. The sights, sounds and aromas of that game are indelible in my mind forever.

There were some lean years to come later in the '70s. There were the free agent signing busts (Stennett, Trillo, etc.). There were increased parking, ticket and concession prices. There were the arctic cold nights. There were the flakey players. There were the threats of selling the franchise and moving to another city, which happened on more than one occasion.

I do not necessarily care for the direction that the game of baseball has taken in recent years, through free agency, expansion, strikes, the Pete Rose saga, steroids and all of the other on and off field controversies that have transpired. But, I do still love, appreciate and respect the game itself. It endures regardless. I do not let any player or political issue stand above it. I certainly do not let it affect the memories of what has transpired on that field.

There is something special about getting your day started and going to the park. I often go to the game early, just to sit in a park that is relatively empty. For me, there is solitude. The serenity cannot be matched; in a few hours, the place will be buzzing.

For 40 years, our patience was tested with the winter-like conditions of Candlestick Park. We were consistently challenged by the weather, balancing our love of the game with how many sweaters we could muster to wear. Now, with AT&T Park (Pacific Bell / SBC Park), we have baseball Shangri-La. I never thought that I would see and experience a baseball Mecca such as this in my life in San Francisco.

Prior to the Giants departure of Candlestick Park, most local news organizations started their "top ten" moments lists. These consisted of a ranking of all the most memorable games or moments played there. After looking at these, I realized that I was in attendance for about seven of them. It started me to think and reflect. Then I started to jot down more memorable moments that I witnessed. Then I realized that each of these moments also had a story. Since I was there, I decided that I wanted to share the stories.

Originally, I wanted to capture the **entire** history of the San Francisco Giants. I did not just want to record a history of the team, but wanted to document the **complete** history. This would have included all lists, statistics and sundry information. That is a tall order and would be quite voluminous. Then I realized that all of that had been done before. If I followed that path, the work would become an almanac or encyclopedia. I wanted to create a different body of work. At that point, the storyteller came out of me.

This project has allowed me to write about many of my first-hand accounts. In many cases, these are some of the defining moments in team history. I have been fortunate to be a witness to this history.

To tell the stories, it was not as difficult as you may think. I have been a fan of this team since the age of six. I started reading the *San Francisco Chronicle* Sporting Green in the first grade and have not stopped since and now read four sports papers and view numerous informational websites, each day. The thirst for more and more information about the Giants has endured. I have become a self-proclaimed historian of the team.

Growing up just 10 minutes from Candlestick Park allowed me to spend many, many years watching my favorite team. In some cases, with just hundreds of my closest friends in the seemingly frigid ice box we called home. It was a dump, but it was our dump.

There were the memories that true fans will never forget. There were real sunny days (contrary to popular belief). There were the no-hitters. There were the comebacks. There were the grand slams. There were the World Series games. There was even a major earthquake.

We had Mays, McCovey, Perry, Marichal, both Bonds and both Clarks. We have had Kruk, Kuip, Speier, Montefusco, Lavelle, Beck, Williams and Nen. We have had Bailey, Barton, Chavez, Pitlock, Pettini, Martin, Novoa and Spradlin.

We have had memories of the beautiful game of baseball; for 50 years, we have had a fountain of them. Join me as we celebrate the San Francisco Giants' golden anniversary.

Chapter 1: The Move West (1958)

1958: The Giants Move West from New York

At the end of the 1957 season, the New York Giants startled their fans by announcing that the franchise was moving west to San Francisco for the 1958 season. Amid much controversy and emotion, Giants' owner Horace Stoneham decided to relocate his team 3,000 miles away after nearly 75 years in New York. The Giants had experienced poor attendance that was dwindling for several seasons. Attendance had fallen from 1.2 million in the World Championship season of 1954 to less than 633,000 in 1956. With the Polo Grounds slated to be demolished and replaced by a housing development, the team was looking for a new home. Stoneham's decision was purely financial as he saw much more potential economic opportunity in a section of the United States that Major League Baseball had not yet tapped. The Giants' Board of Directors voted eight to one in favor of the move. The team settled in San Francisco and was welcomed with open arms by the city. Initially, there were reports the club would move to Minneapolis, Minnesota, site of their top farm club, the Millers. Stoneham liked the idea of California better because the Giants' mortal rivals, and New York brethren, the Brooklyn Dodgers, were also headed to California, settling in Los Angeles. This brought Major League baseball past the Mississippi River for the first time.

04/15/58: First Major League Baseball Game on the West Coast vs. Los Angeles

The first Major League baseball game played on the West Coast took place at the Giants' temporary home, Seals Stadium, in San Francisco. The Giants' defeated the hated Los Angeles Dodgers 8-0, as Ruben Gomez pitched the team to a six-hit shutout victory. The Giants knocked out the Dodgers' mighty star pitcher Don Drysdale after just 3 2/3 innings. Daryl Spencer and flashy rookie Orlando Cepeda hammered home runs in the 11-hit attack. Cepeda was playing in his first Major League game and hit a home run in his second at-bat. A capacity crowd of 23,192 jammed the stadium to embrace their new team. The Giants' adopted the small stadium, home of the city's one-time Pacific Coast League (Triple-A) team, for two seasons. Ironically, the first batter of the game for the Dodgers, Gino Cimoli, was a native San Franciscian.

Seals Stadium (1958-1959)

Seals Stadium had been the home of the Seals, San Francisco's perennial Pacific Coast League powerhouse, for decades. When it was announced that the Giants would relocate to the city, the Seals packed-up and headed for Vancouver after the 1957 campaign. The park was opened in 1931. Although a minor-league park, it had all the standards of a big-league facility. While the Giants were waiting for their permanent home to be built at Candlestick Point, they played two seasons at the Bryant Street stadium. Seals Stadium had a maximum capacity of approximately 23,500 fans. Many feel that the Giants erred by not ever entertaining the notion of upgrading and adding to the already existing structure for their permanent home, if just from the perspective of better weather.

Orlando Cepeda: 1958 National League Rookie of the Year

Orlando Cepeda was the first rookie star to come along for the Giants after they moved to the West. Cepeda debuted in the teams inaugural year in San Francisco, 1958. He earned the starting first baseman job in Spring Training and went on to a memorable campaign. The powerful Cepeda earned Rookie of the Year honors, unanimously winning the award, with a .312 batting average, 25 home runs and 96 runs batted in. A real favorite of then owner Horace Stoneham, Cepeda was considered the Giants' best prospect to come along since Willie Mays in the early '50s.

Horace Stoneham, Owner

Giants' owner Horace Stoneham had the reputation of being a shrewd businessman with a proficiency for living the high life. When it came to baseball, Stoneham also had a sharp mind and consummated numerous deals that strengthened his club and brought them National League Pennants in 1951, 1954 and 1962. He was also a pioneer in scouting the Latin American and Caribbean countries for the immense untapped talent that resided in those nations; the Giants signed numerous star players during the '50s and '60s and integrated their teams. Stoneham also made the very difficult decision to relocate his franchise from New York to San Francisco for the 1958 season.

07/30/59: Willie McCovey's 4-for-4 Major League Debut vs. Philadelphia

Young prospect Willie McCovey was hitting .372 with 29 home runs and 92 runs batted in at AAA Phoenix (PCL) when he was promoted to the big club in mid-summer, 1959 (McCovey still won the PCL league crowns in both categories). Having played both ends of a doubleheader the previous day and traveling all night with little sleep, manager

Bill Rigney placed McCovey in the starting lineup on that Thursday afternoon, July 30. Showing no signs of being weary, McCovey began his remarkable career with a bang as he went a perfect 4-for-4 in a 7-2 Giants' victory over the Philadelphia Phillies and future Hall-of-Fame pitcher Robin Roberts at Seals Stadium. McCovey's four hits included two triples. Willie became the first player to obtain four hits in his first game since Casey Stengel in 1912. A few days later, on August 2, McCovey smashed the first of his 521 career home runs off Pirate pitcher Ron Kline. Voted the favorite 1950s Memory by fans in a website ballot vote in 2003.

Willie McCovey: 1959 National League Rookie of the Year

Although McCovey joined the Giants in the middle of the 1959 season and played in just 52 games, Willie had a spectacular two-month stretch (no pun intended) where he batted .354 and had 13 home runs and 38 runs batted in. His performance impressed everyone throughout the league and he garnered the 1959 National League Rookie of the Year Award. Like his teammate Orlando Cepeda the previous season, McCovey was a unanimous selection for the honor.

Chapter 2: A New Home and Establishment (1960)

Candlestick Park: Part One - Location, Construction, George Christopher, etc.

The birth of Candlestick Park actually started in 1954 when the voters of San Francisco approved a $5 million bond issue to finance a new stadium. Mayor George Christopher lured owner Horace Stoneham and his Giants to San Francisco with the promise of a superb 40,000 seat modern stadium. Construction magnate Charles Harney owned a large parcel of land on the edge of San Francisco, on the Bay, which was over 40 acres in size. He sold this land to the city and his company completed all the construction. Groundbreaking for the stadium commenced in 1958. From its very beginning, Candlestick Park would always seem to find itself surrounded by controversy.

Candlestick Park: Part Two - First of the New Parks

In April, 1960, San Francisco's new baseball stadium opened for play. It was named Candlestick Park, the winning moniker having been chosen through a contest held the year before. It was the first new stadium built in the United States since the Great Depression of the 1930s. Its design, characteristics and substance made it state-of-the-art for its time. Candlestick Park was the first in a long line of the new "concrete and steel" symmetrical stadiums that were built in the '60s and '70s. The park quickly fell under harsh criticism because of its poor location. The open outfield allowed icy winds to whip in from the Bay, which often dropped the already cool temperatures an additional 15 to 20 degrees during the course of a night game. The park's design originally called for radiant heat/steam heating to be provided in pipes buried in the concrete beneath the stands. That feature never worked and efforts to repair were eventually scrapped.

Candlestick Park: Part Three - Full Enclosure, Astroturf and Back to Grass

In order to lure San Francisco's professional football team, the 49ers, Candlestick Park was renovated and became a fully enclosed stadium in 1971. Capacity was increased to over 62,000. The 49ers had played in decrepit Kezar Stadium on the edge of Golden Gate Park for 25 seasons. It was no longer serviceable and Candlestick Park became their new home. In addition, as in many stadiums across America, an artificial surface known as Astroturf was installed. This remained in place for the 1971-1978 seasons. For the 1979 season, to the delight of all players, Kentucky bluegrass was replanted.

04/12/60: Opening Game at Candlestick Park vs. St. Louis

The Giants played the inaugural game in Candlestick Park, against the St. Louis Cardinals. The sellout crowd of 42,269 included Vice President Richard M. Nixon who threw out the ceremonial first pitch. Sam Jones pitched a three-hitter for a 3-1 Giants' victory. Ex-Giant Leon "Daddy Wags" Wagner clubbed the first home run in the new park. In the third inning, the umpires noticed an error in the logistical layout of the field. They protested that the foul poles were several inches (or entirely) into

fair territory, rather than on the foul lines. The Giants did not make the correction until after the completion of the first season.

07/19/60: Juan Marichal Major League Debut (One-Hit Shutout) vs. Philadelphia

When he was signed out of the Dominican Air Force at age 19, high-kicking Juan Marichal already had pinpoint control of his curve, slider, screwball, and blinding fastball, all thrown with a variety of motions. He had led the 1958 Midwest League and the 1959 Eastern League in wins and earned-run average. He debuted his magnificent career with the Giants on July 19, 1960. Juan had one of the most memorable debut performances for any pitcher in history by throwing a complete game, one-hit shutout against the Philadelphia Phillies. The Phillies' lone hit, a single, came off the bat of catcher turned pinch-hitter Clayton Dalrymple in the eighth inning. Marichal, the "Dominican Dandy," struck out 12 and won the game 2-0. Four days later, Marichal four-hit the soon-to-be World Champion Pittsburgh Pirates.

Giants First Tour of Japan: October / November, 1960

The link between professional baseball in the United States and Japan dates back to the mid-nineteenth century. Major league teams began touring Japan in 1913. These ventures have always occurred in the fall, after baseball's postseason. At the end of the 1960 season, the San Francisco Giants traveled to Japan for the first time. That team was led by veteran Willie Mays, with a supporting cast that included back-to-back Rookie of the Year winners Orlando Cepeda and Willie McCovey.

The team had a two-day stopover in Hawaii for two games against the Hawaiian All-Stars first and won those decisively 5-1 and 7-0. In the opener in Japan, the first of a sixteen-game exhibition series, the Giants lost to their Tokyo counterparts, 1-0, and they lost again the next day, 2-1, to the Japanese All-Stars. The team then rebounded and finished with an impressive eleven wins, four losses, and one tie for the month-long tour. At that time, many felt that the one-month tour, though the norm, was too long and that two weeks would have been sufficient.

The 1960 tour was special for another reason: baseball great Lefty O'Doul traveled with the Giants as an honorary coach, though he had formally retired from the game. O'Doul is considered by many to be the "Father of Japanese Baseball" for his diplomatic efforts promoting the game before and after World War II. He was enshrined into the Japanese Baseball Hall-of-Fame in 2001 (although he is not a member of the U.S. National Baseball Hall-of-Fame in Cooperstown).

Mays was named the Most Valuable Player of the tour by a committee of managers and officials. Willie was 23-for-57 for a .404 batting average and clubbed seven home runs. He was awarded a Japanese automobile.

Chapter 3: Early Success (1960-62)

04/30/61: Willie Mays' Four Home Runs in One Game at Milwaukee

Using teammate Joey Amalfitano's bat, Willie Mays became the ninth player in Major League history to smash four home runs in a nine-inning game. On the day, Mays put on one of the most memorable demonstrations in baseball history. His eight runs batted in paced the Giants to a 14-4 win at Milwaukee. All the home runs were impressive, but Willie's sixth-inning home run was monstrous as it cleared the left field bleachers at County Stadium. Willie nearly stroked a fifth home run midway through the game that was caught at the centerfield wall by Hank Aaron. In addition, fans booed Giant third baseman Jim Davenport as he made the final out in the top of the ninth inning, leaving Mays in the on deck circle and extinguishing his chance for five home runs in the contest. Home Run King Hank Aaron collected a pair of home runs, accounting for all of the Braves' scoring.

04/30/61: Most Home Runs by a Team in a Game (Eight) at Milwaukee (Tie)

In the very same game that Willie Mays hit his record-tying four home runs, the Giants tied a Major League record for home runs by one team in a game with eight round trippers. Jose Pagan added two home runs, and Felipe Alou and Orlando Cepeda contributed one each. Combined with the five home runs they hit the previous day, the Giants also equaled the Major League record for home runs in two consecutive games, with 13. The Giants had been no-hit by the legendary Warren Spahn just two days prior.

1961 All-Star Game at Candlestick Park

On July 11, 1961, in just the stadium's second year of existence, the Giants hosted the first of their two All-Star Games at Candlestick Park. Candlestick Park always had the reputation as being the coldest and windiest place to play baseball in the world. Strong winds dominated play throughout the contest. A crowd of 44,115 chilled fans were on hand to see the National League defeat the American League by a score of 5-4. Hometown hero Willie Mays blasted a double in the 10th inning to drive in the tying run. He then scored the winning run on Roberto Clemente's single. The game may be best remembered for the gust of wind that knocked Giants' relief pitcher Stu Miller off the mound with runners at first and second base in the ninth inning. The umpire had no choice but to call a balk. This enabled the American League to forge a 3-3 tie, before losing in 10 innings.

08/23/61: Most Home Runs (Team) in One Inning (Five) vs. Cincinnati (Tie)

In the ninth inning of a long August, 1961 night game at Cincinnati, the Giants potent lineup erupted for five home runs on their way to a 14-0 victory over the Reds. This tied the Major League record for home runs in an inning. Orlando Cepeda, Felipe Alou, John Orsino, Willie Mays and Jim Davenport all contributed four-baggers in the one-sided offensive onslaught. Davenport's home run was an inside-the-park hit; Cepeda and Willie McCovey each collected two hits in that same ninth inning.

1961: Stu Miller Amasses 14 Wins in Relief

One of the best relief pitchers of the early San Francisco Giants was Stu Miller. He provided effective support out of the bullpen during the 1961 season, amassing a remarkable 14 wins in relief, while appearing in 67 games. He also tied for the league lead in saves with 17. Miller was selected to play in both 1961 All-Star Games and pitched a total of 4 2/3 innings, yielding no earned runs, one hit and striking out nine. In the game hosted by the Giants, he earned the win in relief.

"Sad" Sam Jones, Career

Sam Jones was the Giants' first 20-game winner in San Francisco. A real workhorse, Jones tied for the National League lead in wins (21) in 1959 while leading the circuit in earned-run average at 2.83. He also led the 1960 team in wins with 18. Over his three-year career with the Giants, Jones amassed 47 wins and had an earned run average of 3.30. Often called a "hard luck pitcher," Jones lost three no-hit bids after the seventh inning while pitching for the Giants during his career. Hence, he picked up the nickname "Sad." Jones was also known as "Toothpick." Sam began his career in the Negro Leagues.

Jack Sanford: 16-Game Winning Streak in 1962

On September 11, 1962 Jack Sanford shutout the Pittsburgh Pirates 2-0 for his remarkable 16th consecutive win. In mid-season, Sanford was in a real pitching groove where he did not lose a single game between

June 17 and September 11. Sanford went on to compile a 24-7 record for the year and led the Giants to the National League Pennant. Sanford gave the Giants their first World Series victory in San Francisco, a 2-0 masterpiece against the Yankees in Game 2 at Candlestick Park. Pitching on just two days rest, he held the powerful Bronx Bombers to just three hits.

10/01-03/62: Best-of-Three National League Pennant Sudden Death Playoff vs. Los Angeles

The Giants of 1962 were four full games behind the Los Angeles Dodgers in mid-September in the National League standings; the team then scratched and fought its way into a tie during the final two weeks of the campaign. In order to decide the league champion, a best-of-three playoff series was slated for October 1-3, with the winner receiving the Pennant and a bid to play in the World Series. The Giants won the playoff two games to one and concluded it in dramatic comeback fashion in the deciding Game 3. The Giants staged a four-run rally in the ninth inning at Los Angeles, and vaulted into the Series. They are considered by many experts to perhaps be the best all-around team in San Francisco history.

A brief summary of the exciting and memorable three-game playoff series:

Game 1 at Candlestick Park, 10/01/62

In Game 1 at Candlestick Park, Billy Pierce earned his 12th straight win at home with a dominant three-hit, 8-0 victory. Willie Mays hit two home runs, giving him 49 for the year, one more than American League leader Harmon Killebrew. Sandy Koufax, making just his third start since returning from a hand injury, was the loser, pitching just one inning. A crowd of 32,660 was on hand.

Game 2 at Dodger Stadium, 10/02/62

Just 25,321 fans showed up at Dodger Stadium to see Los Angeles ace Don Drysdale (25-9) and Jack Sanford (24-7) square off. The Giants sprinted to a 5-0 lead early. However, after 35 consecutive scoreless innings, the Dodgers broke through for seven runs in the bottom of the sixth inning to lead the Giants by two runs. The Giants scored twice in the eighth, but a ninth-inning sacrifice fly by Ron Fairly sent Maury Wills home with the winning run and an 8-7 victory. The Giants tied a National League record by using eight pitchers in a nine-inning game. At four hours and 18 minutes, the game was also the longest nine-inning contest in National League history at the time.

Game 3 at Dodger Stadium, 10/03/62

For the third and deciding game, a more robust crowd of 45,693 gave the Dodgers a Major League single-season attendance record of 2,755,184. In the seventh inning, Maury Wills collected his fourth single of the day, and his 103rd and 104th stolen bases of the year. The Giants countered with an amazing comeback by scoring four runs in the ninth inning to win 6-4 and an appearance in the World Series against the vaunted New York Yankees. Like 11 years earlier in the Polo Grounds, the Giants were not to be denied, as a Willie Mays single cut the deficit to 4-3. Orlando Cepeda tied the score with a sacrifice fly and Jim Davenport drew a bases loaded walk that brought home the eventual winning run. Billy Pierce, appearing in relief, retired the Dodgers in the bottom of the ninth inning for the save, and the Giants had a 6-4 victory. The game was voted the favorite 1960s Memory by fans in a website ballot vote in 2003.

1962 National League Champions

For 1962, the Giants assembled possibly the best team in franchise history. They set a record for wins in a season with 103 (including playoffs / tied by the 1993 team). New manager Alvin Dark boasted a club that had five future Hall-of-Famers: Mays, McCovey, Marichal, Perry and Cepeda. Mays clubbed 49 home runs, while Cepeda added 35 and Felipe Alou smashed 25. The pitching staff was mighty, with the four starters totaling 77 wins: Sanford (24), O'Dell (19), Marichal (18), and Pierce (16). Unsung heroes Davenport, Pagan, Hiller and Haller provided solid defense. Stu Miller was the top fireman with 19 saves and veteran Don Larsen provided good support out of the bullpen. The team had solid months in April (15W-5L) and May (20W-10L).

10/08/62: Chuck Hiller - First National League World Series Grand Slam Home Run vs. New York Yankees

Because he started the final playoff game against the Dodgers, San Francisco ace Juan Marichal was not able to start in the World Series until Game 4. Marichal was excellent, tossing four scoreless innings, but he was forced to leave the game after suffering a hand injury while batting in the top of the fifth inning. His replacements held on until the seventh inning, when Giant second baseman Chuck Hiller smashed a surprising grand slam home run to give his club a 6-2 lead. The final score was 7-3, and the World Series was evened at two games apiece. Hiller, who hit only 20 home runs in his entire eight-year Major League career, took center stage when he walloped a bases-full home run off Yankee's reliever Marshall Bridges. The grand slam, the first in World Series history by a National League player, snapped a 2-2 tie at Yankee Stadium and made a winner out of a 33-year-old San Francisco reliever who had retired only one batter in the game. Ironically, that well-traveled pitcher was one Don Larsen, who six years before, to the very day, had pitched the only perfect game in World Series history for the Yankees against Brooklyn in the same park.

1962 World Series vs. New York Yankees

In their first World Series in San Francisco, the Giants took the mighty New York Yankees to the final out in the bottom of the ninth inning of Game 7. The Giants kept the series alive with excellent pitching performances from Jack Sanford, Juan Marichal, and Billy Pierce. Finally in Game 7, with the winning runs on base, Willie McCovey belted a hard liner toward second base that Bobby Richardson snagged and ended the game and series. In the seventh and deciding game for the world title, New York scored the game's only run, as Tony Kubek grounded into a fifth inning double play. The Giants' did not die without first providing some drama. In the ninth inning, Matty Alou led off with a bunt single. The next two hitters struck out and Matty Alou was still stranded on first base. Willie Mays ripped a double to right field off Ralph Terry. Courtesy of wet ground and great fielding by Roger Maris, Alou was held at third base by coach Whitey Lockman and kept from scoring. With Willie McCovey due up and Orlando Cepeda on deck, Yankee manager Ralph Houk asked Terry who he would rather face. They decided on McCovey. After blasting a home run foul, the hard-hitting left hander sent a screaming liner toward short right field. Reliable second baseman Bobby Richardson gloved it, giving the Yankees a 1-0 win and their second straight World Series victory. Because of uncharacteristically heavy rain, the series was drawn out for 13 days. The Giants had slightly better statistics for the series than the Yankees out hitting them .226 to .199 and having a better earned run average, 2.66 versus 2.95.

"Bye, Bye Baby": San Francisco Giants' Fight Song

Russ Hodges, the legendary "Voice of the Giants" for 22 seasons in New York and San Francisco, coined the phrase, "bye-bye baby," to describe a home run hit by the hometown favorites. In many ways, that catchy slogan has exemplified the persona of the San Francisco Giants' team and its fans for nearly 50 years. It has been synonymous with the Giant image, and the very essence of the franchise. It can still be heard today on television broadcasts and at the ballpark.

Here are the lyrics:

When the Giants come to town, it's "Bye-Bye Baby!"
Every time the chips are down, it's "Bye-Bye Baby!"
History's in the making at Candlestick Park!
Cheer for the batter, and light the spark!
If you're a fan of Giants' baseball, sing "Bye-Bye Baby!"
If you want to be in first place, call "Bye-Bye Baby!"
Listen to the broadcast on KSFO.
Turn up the volume, and hear 'em go.
With the San Francisco Giants, it's "Bye-Bye Baby!"

Chapter 4: Consistently Second Place (1963-1970)

06/15/63: Juan Marichal No-Hitter vs. Houston

Young Juan Marichal hurled the first no-hitter in San Francisco Giants' history. This was the first for the franchise in over 34 years (Carl Hubbell on May 8, 1929). Juan was also first Latin-American pitcher to throw a no-hitter in the Major Leagues. Marichal's effort helped the Giants to a 1-0 victory over the Houston Colt .45s before a crowd of 18,869 at Candlestick Park. Chuck Hiller's two-out double in the eighth inning scored Jim Davenport from second base for the lone run. Marichal needed only 89 pitches to finish off Houston, but his teammates were finding it equally difficult to break through on the scoreboard. The no-hitter was saved with a great defensive play by Willie McCovey in left field. McCovey was an outfielder early in his career, and not known for his defense. He caught a ball at the fence hit by the .45's Carl Warwick and saved the day for Juan. The Giants managed only three hits themselves for the game.

07/02/63: Marichal vs. Spahn (Milwaukee) and a 16-Inning Pitching Duel

On June 15, 1963, Marichal no-hit Houston 1-0. A little over two weeks later on July 2, he engaged Hall-of-Fame pitcher Warren Spahn in a memorable and epic pitching battle that can only be described as a "duel." Marichal and Spahn battled for an amazing 16 innings in one of the most memorable games in Giants' history. Both pitchers tossed complete games in the brisk air (although the middle of summer of Candlestick Park. A crowd of 15,921 was in attendance for the game that ended at 12:31 a.m. With zeros on the board, Spahn escaped a bases-loaded jam in the bottom of the 14th inning and retired Harvey Kuenn to start of the 16th. Willie Mays finally ended the affair with a walk-off home run.

It was a long night. Many felt that the game had ended in the bottom of the ninth inning when Willie McCovey belted one of his clutch home runs down the right field line. Umpire Chris Pelekoudas disagreed and called it a foul ball and the game continued. In the end, both pitchers posted impressive numbers: Marichal tossed 16 innings (227 pitches), gave up eight hits, walked four and fanned 11; Spahn pitched 15 1/3 innings (201 pitches), surrendered nine hits, walked one and struck out two. The one walk was intentional, to Willie Mays. Mays ended Spahn's streak of 27 consecutive shutout innings with the home run. After nine innings, Milwaukee manager Bobby Bragen asked Spahn to come out of the game. Spahn refused. On the other side of the field, Giants manager Alvin Dark also suggested that Marichal give way to the bullpen. Marichal too, refused. Juan entered the game with an eight-game win streak and a 12-3 record. Spahn was 42 years old at the time but showed no signs of old age; he entered the game with an 11-3 record and five straight victories.

07/09/63: Willie Mays All-Star Game Most Valuable Player

Willie Mays showed his sterling all-around baseball ability by helping the National League to a 5-3 victory, with his bat and glove, at Cleveland in the 1963 All-Star Game. Willie went 1-for-3, drove in two runs, scored two runs, stole two bases, and made the defensive play of the game in the eighth inning by robbing Joe Pepitone of extra bases. For his efforts, Mays was named the Most Valuable Player. Surprisingly, the American League out-hit the National League 11-6. Willie was held to a single but dominated the National League win, as he put on a one-man show.

05/31/64: The Longest Day - at New York (N) (Two Games, 32 Innings, Almost 10 Hours of Baseball)

The Giants and the New York Mets were scheduled to play a doubleheader, but by the time their day was over they played a great deal more. The entire twinbill lasted 32 innings and took an astonishing nine hours and 52 minutes to complete. This is the longest in Major League history. The second game itself was the longest game in National League history (by time) with 23 innings encompassing an astounding seven hours and 23 minutes. The Giants won both games, 5-3 in the opener and 8-6 in the second. The Giants held a 6-1 lead in the second game, only to have the Mets rally to tie it in the bottom of the seventh inning 6-6. From there, goose eggs adorned the scoreboard for a long time until the Giants broke through. An overflow crowd of 57,037 jammed Shea Stadium for the doubleheader. The last out was made at precisely 11:24 p.m. allowing everyone to go home and sleep. Luckily, the Giants had the next day off, while they traveled to Pittsburgh. The day was weird enough by itself, but there were more oddities that transpired on this day, as well. Here are a few examples:

- In the opener, Orlando Cepeda stole home. In the second game, Cepeda hit into a double play and also hit into a triple play.
- Willie Mays played part of Game 2 at shortstop.

♦ Giants' manager Alvin Dark was ejected in the 15th inning of Game 2 and had to manage the remainder of the game, which took several hours, from a restroom behind the dugout, while standing on a commode.

♦ Young Gaylord Perry pitched 10 innings of shutout relief and struck out 10 to gain the win in the nightcap.

Masanori Murakami: First Japanese Player in Major League Baseball (1964-1965)

The left-handed Masanori Murakami was the first Japanese native to play Major League Baseball. Murakami showed great promise as a 19 year-old pitcher while a member of the 1964 Fresno Giants (Class A). There he had an 11-7 record, 1.78 earned-run average and 15 saves. His strong performance earned him a late-season promotion to the San Francisco club where he pitched in nine games in late 1964. In 1965, he appeared in 45 games and had a very impressive 4-1 record. An agreement could not be reached for the 1966 season, and Murakami returned to his native country and continued his career for the Nankai Hawks in the Japanese League. A true pioneer, not for over three more decades would Japanese players appear in mass on Major League rosters.

07/13/65: Juan Marichal All-Star Game Most Valuable Player

Giants' star pitcher Juan Marichal started the All-Star Game for the National League at Minnesota. Marichal pitched three scoreless innings and yielded just one lone hit, allowed no runs and did not walk a batter in earning Most Valuable Player honors. Marichal also went 1-for-1 at the plate and scored a run, helping the National League to a 6-5 victory. Willie Mays sparked the offense with a leadoff home run that traveled 415 feet. He also scored what was the winning run in the seventh inning.

Frank Linzy: 1965 *Sporting News* National League Rookie of the Year

After a brief stint with the club in 1963, Frank Linzy appeared on the scene for 1965 providing great support out of the bullpen and was the leading reliever for the team. Linzy appeared in 57 games, won nine, saved 21, and had a magnificent 1.43 earned-run average. For his efforts, Linzy was named the 1965 *Sporting News* National League Rookie of the Year. Linzy wore a Giants' uniform for the better part of seven seasons until his trade in 1970.

Jack Sanford, Career

Jack Sanford's strong pitching in 1962 helped the Giants to their first San Francisco World Series appearance. Sanford appeared in 39 games, pitched 265 innings, and had a 24-7 record. After starting the season 6-6 Sanford went 18-1, including winning a club-record 16 straight. During his seven-year career with the Giants, Sanford won 89 games, pitched nine shutouts (including a league leading six in 1960) and had an earned run average of 3.61.

Willie Mays: 1965 National League Most Valuable Player

Willie Mays had one of the best overall years of his career and won his second National League Most Valuable Player award in 1965. Willie batted .317, hit a career high 52 home runs and drove in 112 runs. Mays smacked a remarkable 17 home runs during the month of August to put the Giants in contention for the Pennant.

05/04/66: Willie Mays Establishes the National League Career Home Run Record (512)

Willie Mays hammered his 512th career home run off of Dodgers' pitcher Claude Osteen to set the National League career record on May 4, 1966. Osteen was normally stingy when it came to roundtrippers and Mays had been slumping horribly prior to the clout, in the midst of a 3-23 drought. His blast broke the record previously held by New York Giant slugging great Mel Ott. The home run put him behind only Babe Ruth, Ted Williams, and Jimmy Foxx, at that point, on the all-time home run list.

Orlando Cepeda, Career

Orlando Cepeda was a regular in the Giants' lineup, whether he played first base or the outfield, during most of his nine seasons with the team. After winning National League Rookie of the Year honors in 1958, Cepeda had another monster campaign in 1961 when he belted 46 home runs, drove in 142 and batted .311. Cepeda also had a great year in 1962 and helped the Giants to the World Series. A knee injury sidelined him for a large part of the 1965 season and he was eventually traded to St. Louis as the Giants looked for more pitching support and had another slugger to play first base, Willie McCovey. Cepeda is in the Top-10 of most career offensive categories for San Francisco. Nicknamed the "Baby Bull" and "Cha Cha." Cepeda was selected as a member of the All-1960s Team and the All-Time San Francisco Giant Team in 1999. He was elected to the Baseball Hall-of-Fame in 1999.

Mike McCormick: 1967 National League Cy Young Award Winner

Though the Giants have had many star pitchers during their tenure in San Francisco, surprisingly, Mike McCormick is the only one to garner the prestigious Cy Young Award, doing so in 1967. McCormick was an original Giant "bonus-baby" and was then traded after the 1962 season. Mike returned in 1967 to have a strong year in which he had a league-leading 22-10 record, pitched 262 1/3 innings, and had a 2.85 earned-run average. He also had 14 complete games and five shutouts. Interestingly enough, McCormick did not win his first game until May 4, but was 11-3 by the All-Star break and won eight consecutive decisions in June and July. McCormick was also named the National League Comeback Player of the Year.

06/25/68: Bobby Bonds' Major League Debut vs. Los Angeles (Grand Slam)

Bobby Bonds made his Major League debut in grand fashion. Bonds smashed a grand slam home run off John Purdin in the sixth inning, helping the Giants pummel the rival Dodgers 9-0 at Los Angeles. This was the first grand slam by a rookie in his first Major League game since 1898. Ray Sadecki tossed a two-hitter for the win. Bonds went on to a very successful career with the Giants and was a fan favorite until his trade to the Yankees at the conclusion of the 1974 season.

07/09/68: Willie Mays All-Star Game Most Valuable Player

The 1968 All-Star Game was unique because it was the first-ever played indoors or on an artificial surface. It also marked the first 1-0 game in history. Two Giants sluggers played a role in the scoring of the lone run as pitching dominated the game. Willie Mays, playing in place of injured Pete Rose, tallied an unearned run in the first inning against American League starter Luis Tiant to complete the scoring for the day. Mays led off the bottom of the first with a single, and took second when first baseman Harmon Killebrew mishandled Tiant's pickoff throw for an error. Mays took third as the rattled Tiant threw a wild pitch to walk Curt Flood, and scored when fellow Giants' slugger Willie

McCovey grounded into a routine double play. Mays was named the Most Valuable Player. Marichal pitched two hitless innings.

09/17/68: Gaylord Perry No-Hitter vs. St. Louis

Gaylord Perry hurled the second Giants' no-hitter of the decade as he defeated the St. Louis Cardinals at Candlestick Park. The Giants edged the Cardinals and Bob Gibson 1-0. Ron Hunt's solo home run backed Perry, who evened his record at 14-14. Perry struck out nine and walked two in the 101-itch performance. The entire effort took only one hour and 40 minutes to complete. A crowd of 9,546 saw the masterpiece. Bob Gibson, in his record breaking season, took the loss, allowing only four hits and striking out 10.

The Alou Brothers: Matty, Felipe and Jesus

Felipe (1958-63), Jesus (1963-68), and Matty (1960-65) were fixtures in the Giant lineup during the 1960s. The Alou brothers were scouted and signed in the baseball talent-rich country of the Dominican Republic. The trio provided support both in the starting lineup and off the bench. History was made on September 15, 1963 when all three Alou brothers appeared in the Giant outfield in the same inning at Pittsburgh. Felipe went on to manage the club.

Most Giant's Pitching Wins at Home and on the Road for a Season

In 1968, Juan Marichal had a sensational season, posting a career and San Francisco franchise-high 26 wins. He started a total of 38 games, and completed an amazing 30 of them. The most unbelievable statistic from this season is that Marichal was 18-4 on the road for the year. Today, this gaudy figure is not even approached by many starters for an entire season, home and road. The franchise record for home wins in a season is 15 by "Sad" Sam Jones in 1960. Jones was not nearly as successful on the road, having an 18-14 overall record that year.

07/23/69: Willie McCovey All-Star Game Most Valuable Player

In the midst of the best groove of his career, Willie McCovey provided a big spark for the National League in the All-Star Game, slugging two home runs, driving in three runs and scoring two runs in a 9-3 victory over the American League at Washington. For his efforts, McCovey was named the game's Most Valuable Player. After four one-run victories in a row, the National League finally broke loose, amassing 10 of their 11 hits in the first four innings for nine runs and a crushing win. McCovey's two-run home run began the third inning scoring. Willie hit another home run again in the fourth inning for the Nationals' final tally. McCovey's home runs were off John "Blue Moon" Odom of Oakland and Denny McLain of Detroit.

09/22/69: Willie Mays 600th Career Home Run at San Diego

Willie Mays joined just Babe Ruth in the 600 Home Run Club with a seventh inning blast off Mike Corkins, while pinch-hitting for rookie George Foster. San Francisco beat San Diego 4-2. Oddly, Corkins was taken from San Francisco by the Padres in the 1968 expansion draft. Mays had sat out the game as a starter because he had been pressing for the historic hit. With one on in a tie game, Mays belted a drive to deep left-center field over the 385-foot marker into empty bleachers. The sparse crowd of less than 5,000 gave him a standing ovation.

Juan Marichal: The 1960's Most Dominant Pitcher (191 Wins)

During the decade of the 1960s, several pitchers asserted themselves in the upper echelon of the National League. Names like Gibson, Koufax, Drysdale and Carlton come to mind. However, the Giants' Juan Marichal won more games in the decade than any other Major League hurler, with an amazing 191 wins (Gibson was distant second with 164 wins). Marichal posted 20 or more wins in six of seven consecutive seasons and had an earned-run average in the 2.00 range every year. In 1968 he won a San Francisco franchise-record 26 games. Marichal also led the National League in wins, earned-run average and complete games at various times. Despite all of his success, Marichal never won a Cy Young Award.

Willie Mays: *Sporting News* 1960s Baseball Player of the Decade

Although the competition was extremely tough, perhaps the stiffest for any 10 year span in the history of the game, *The Sporting News* named Willie Mays the 1960s Baseball Player of the Decade. The '60s decade is considered by many to be the best, coupled with the '50s, within the "Golden Age" of the game. Described as a "hero for the working class," Mays was perhaps the best all-around player ever. He was certainly one of the most talented and blessed five-tool players that could do it all on the field. At his peak, Mays could run, hit for average, hit for power, throw and field better than any of his peers. Mays' 350 home runs during the decade is the ninth most in any decade in history.

Willie McCovey: 1969 National League Most Valuable Player

Willie McCovey enjoyed the finest all-around year of his career in 1969. He batted .320, smacked 45 home runs, and drove in 126 runs, all career highs. McCovey easily won the National League's Most Valuable Player. 1969 established him as a true star and solidified his place as one of the true sluggers of the game for his generation and all-time.

Broadcaster: Russ Hodges

Hall-of-Fame broadcaster Russ Hodges began his career calling games for the New York Giants in 1949. He is perhaps best remembered for his call of the 1951 "shot heard around the world" home run by Bobby Thomson versus the Brooklyn Dodgers. Hodges moved West with the team in 1958 and broadcast the first-ever game on the West Coast. He was famous for his home run call "bye-bye baby" which was the inspiration for one of the most famous Giants' anthems. Hodges died suddenly of a heart attack in 1971.

Jimmy Davenport, Career

It can truly be said that Jim Davenport is a cornerstone of the San Francisco Giants organization. During his tenure with the club, he has played, coached, managed, scouted and instructed. Davenport spent 13 years as a player with the team, making his debut in 1958. He is regarded by many as the finest defensive infielder in San Francisco history. Davenport is also in the all-time Top-10 in many San Francisco offensive categories, including fourth in games played. Selected as a member of the All-1960s San Francisco Giant team in 1999.

Ron Hunt: Hit-By-Pitch King

Ron Hunt played his entire Major League career with bruises. He can truly be crowned the all-time "Hit King," hit-by-pitch, that is. His crowded batting stance left no room around home plate. During his career, Hunt was hit 243 times, a National League record. He also holds league records for being hit by pitches for a season (50, 1971), consecutive years leading the league (seven, 1968-74) and HBP in an extra inning game (3). Hunt played 391 games for the Giants.

Spring, 1970: Giants Travel to Japan and Play Nine Exhibition Games

Baseball in the Orient, and specifically Japan, has been popular for decades. Major League players began touring the Far East for exhibitions in the 1930s. The Giants spent part of their 1970 exhibition schedule by traveling to Japan to play the Lotte Orions, Tokyo Giants and other teams of the Japanese Central and Pacific Baseball Leagues. The Giants were the first and only Major League team to tour Japan during Spring Training, in March, **prior** to the start of regular season. The Giants concluded the trip with a disappointing 3-6 record. This was the first, and only, series in which Japanese teams outmatched American Major League competition and emerged with a winning record.

03/21/70: Monumental Game in Tokyo with All-Time Home Run Titans Mays, McCovey and Oh

The Giants opened their nine-game tour of Japan against the Yomiuri Giants (also known as the Tokyo Giants) at Tokyo Stadium. The historic game featured three of the most prolific home run sluggers in the history of professional baseball. Willie Mays and Willie McCovey (San Francisco) and Sadaharu Oh (Tokyo) combined to belt more than 2,000 home runs during their respective careers. Mays and McCovey did not hit any long balls in this game, but Oh had a memorable night, in which the Giants could not get him out. Oh ended the three-hour affair with a home run in the bottom of the 11th inning for a 6-5 Tokyo win. On the night, Oh belted a two-run home run in the first inning, drew a walk in the third, singled in the fifth, got an intentional pass in the seventh, and garnered another walk in the ninth before ending the game with his third hit and run batted in the eleventh. The fences at the stadium were reportedly only 290 feet down the foul lines, but

Oh's clouts left no doubt that he could hit in parks that were much bigger, including those in the United States. Mays ended his career with 660 home runs, McCovey clubbed 521 and Oh holds the all-time professional record with 868 long ones.

KTVU Channel 2 (Oakland): 1970 Satellite Television Broadcast of Historic Game from Japan

During the Giants' tour of Japan, a broadcast event occurred that was one of the most significant in sports history. The Giants' flagship television station, KTVU Channel 2 of Oakland, beamed the game broadcast back to the Bay Area via satellite. This event was a unique first-of-its-kind event, a live colorcast of the San Francisco Giants playing an exhibition game against the Tokyo Giants via satellite from Tokyo Stadium on March 21. The broadcast marked the first baseball game to be broadcast live from a foreign country to the United States, the first time an independent station contracted to use a satellite to serve its own market, and the first time a live telecast had been received directly on the West Coast via satellite. This provided fans with a showcase of what the future of sports viewing would be like. KTVU used the Japanese television feed, with players' names in Japanese and English on the screen, to avoid confusion. KTVU also had a film crew travel with the team and compiled a made-for-television documentary of the trip that aired in the Bay Area just before Opening Day, 1970.

04/11/70: Mays and Bonds - The Catch of the Decade

Willie Mays and Bobby Bonds were part of perhaps one of the most recognizable plays in televised baseball history, one that is forever etched in the mind of many. The Giants were playing the Cincinnati Reds in the NBC "Saturday Game of the Week" early in the 1970 season. Mays, patrolling the outfield in his usual fashion, made one of the most remarkable catches ever seen. Willie was less than one month from his 39th birthday when he ran full speed from his center field position into the gap in right center field at Candlestick Park. Backing toward the cyclone fence, he jumped and soared above the barrier to snag a would-be home run from the bat of Cincinnati's Bobby Tolan. During the play, Mays crashed into right fielder Bobby Bonds (Barry's father) who was also in pursuit, landed with a thud and somehow managed to hold onto the ball. Bonds was knocked-out by Mays' knee hitting his jaw during the play. Prior to Game 4 of the 2002 World Series, Major League Baseball paid tribute to the 10 greatest moments in the game's history as voted upon by fans. When asked about his favorite memory, Giants' slugger Barry Bonds said that his favorite was that very same leaping catch that Mays made. For many years, the scene was used as an introductory clip for NBC's "Game of the Week."

07/18/70: Willie Mays 3,000th Career Hit vs. Montreal

Willie Mays collected the 3,000th base hit of his illustrious career against the Montreal Expos on July 18, 1970 at Candlestick Park. Mays singled to short left field in the second inning off of Expo hurler Mike Wegener, as the Giants trounced the Expos 10-1. Mays became the 10th member of the 3,000 Hit Club. Willie was the first member of the Club to garner the historic feat on the West Coast. The landmark hit came just two months after fellow slugger Hank Aaron of the Braves had joined the Club.

Chapter 5: The Aging Giants (1971-1973)

Spring, 1971: Lotte Orions Travel to the United States and Play the Giants

One year after the Giants traveled to Japan during Spring Training, the Lotte Orions came to Arizona and California to train with several Major League baseball teams. Prior to their departure, the Giants hosted the Orions in a two-game series to close-out the trip in early April at Candlestick Park. The game marked the first time ever that a Japanese team had played on an artificial surface, as Candlestick Park had just been fitted with its new Astroturf. The Orions trounced the Giants on Saturday 9-1. Allowing just three hits, the winning pitcher was Masaaki Koyama, who by the age of 36 had won 290 games in Japan. On Sunday, the Giants bounced back with a 9-4 win. Reserve outfielder Jimmy Rosario became the first man to hit a home run into the newly installed portable football bleachers in right filed at the now-enclosed Candlestick Park.

Giants' Players Shine in Other All-Star Games

As noted, Giants' players have contributed to the success of the National League in the annual All-Star Game each July, over the years. San Francisco has had its share of Most Valuable Players in the Classic. Some of those players and others have played noteworthy roles in games where they were not named the MVP. Here are some other All-Star Game memories:

1959 (Game 1 at Pittsburgh)

Willie Mays hit a run-scoring triple in the bottom of the eighth inning to cap a two-run rally and ensure a 5-4 National League victory in Game 1. Johnny Antonelli pitched 1/3 of an inning and gained the win.

1960 (at Cleveland / New York - A)

In the two All-Star Games this year, Willie Mays went an amazing 6-for-8 (.750). His six hits included a double, a triple and a home run. This helped propel the National League to the only sweep in the four-year history of dual games.

1962 (at Washington)

Juan Marichal pitched in the first of his nine All-Star Games. He hurled two scoreless innings and gained the win as the National League posted a 3-1 victory. Jim Davenport had one hit (single) and Felipe Alou drove in an insurance run with a sacrifice fly in the eighth inning.

1964 (at New York - N)

Juan Marichal won his second All-Star Game at New York's new Shea Stadium. The National League erupted for four runs in the bottom of the ninth inning en route to a 7-4 victory. Willie Mays walked and Orlando Cepeda hit a single during the rally.

1966 (at St. Louis)

Juan Marichal and Gaylord Perry held the American League scoreless over the last five innings to preserve a 2-1 National League win at St. Louis. Perry was the winning pitcher. Willie Mays scored the first run of the game for the National League.

1970 (at Cincinnati)

It took 12 innings to decide, but the National League prevailed as Pete Rose barreled over Cleveland catcher Ray Fosse at home plate for the winning run. Dick Dietz and Willie McCovey had a big role in the 5-4 win. Trailing 4-1 going into the bottom of the ninth inning, the National League rallied to tie the score. Dietz triggered the rally with a lead-off, pinch-hit home run off of Oakland's Jim "Catfish" Hunter and McCovey added a run-scoring single.

1971 (at Detroit)

In his last All-Star Game appearance, Juan Marichal pitched two hitless innings, which included the retiring of three future Hall-of-Famers.

Juan Marichal: Absolute Dominance in All-Star Game Competition

The dominance that Juan Marichal had over the National League during his career has been well documented. It should also be known that he did not discriminate when it came to mowing batters down on the mound. Marichal continued his supremacy over opposing American League hitters in the All-Star Game each time he headed to the hill. In the Mid Summer Classic, his numbers are staggering in terms of their dominance.

In all, Juan pitched in eight games, logged two wins, and had an overall earned run average of just 0.50. He allowed only one earned run and two walks in his 18 innings, equivalent to two full games. After

33

surrendering the lone earned run in his second All-Star appearance, he hurled 14 consecutive scoreless innings over his final seven appearances. He stymied batters to just a paltry .117 batting average and .145 on-base percentage. A review of his stellar numbers in each appearance:

YEAR	G / S	IP	H	R	ER	BB	K	W	L	ERA
1962	2 / 0	4.0	2	2	1	1	2	1	0	2.25
1964	1 / 0	1.0	0	0	0	0	1	1	0	0.00
1965	1 / 1	3.0	1	0	0	0	0	0	0	0.00
1966	1 / 0	3.0	3	0	0	0	2	0	0	0.00
1967	1 / 1	3.0	1	0	0	0	3	0	0	0.00
1968	1 / 0	2.0	0	0	0	0	3	0	0	0.00
1971	1 / 0	2.0	0	0	0	1	1	0	0	0.00
Totals	8 / 2	18.0	7	2	1	2	12	2	0	0.50

OPP B AVG.	OPP OB %
.117	.145

Juan Marichal: Opening Day Dominance for the Giants

With his designation as the team's ace, Marichal also carried supremacy to Opening Day assignments for the G-Men. He earned the prestigious duty for "day one" ten times during his career with San Francisco. Between 1962 and 1973, his statistics included a 6-2 W-L record, six complete games, two shutouts, and a 1.63 earned-run average. His first two decisions were against the famed Warren Spahn, whom he defeated both times. Marichal also helped himself at the plate, as he hit .308 during these contests.

1962 vs. Milwaukee

Young Juan Marichal hurled a three-hit shutout in his first Opening Day assignment. He sent ace Warren Spahn to the showers early, enroute to a 6-0 victory. Spahn lasted just 3 2/3 innings. A crowd of better than

39,000 jammed Candlestick Park to watch the young 24 year old also take the Braves down with his bat. On the day, Marichal had a single and a double, scored two runs and drove in two. Marichal limited the Braves to just one hit until the ninth inning, when Tommy Aaron and Frank Bolling each hit meaningless singles. Marichal fanned 10 Milwaukee hitters, including the feared "Big 3" in the lineup: Hank Aaron three times and Eddie Mathews and Joe Adcock twice each. He completed the game and finished with 10 strikeouts. Willie Mays stroked a home run for the Giants in the very first inning, depositing a 375-foot opposite-field home run over the right-center field fence.

1964 vs. Milwaukee

The "Dominican Dandy" took it to the Braves and Spahn again on this day. Marichal got off to a slow start, yielding four runs in the first three innings (just one earned). He was supported by the Giants' big bats as they rolled out the lumber, striking for five home runs in the contest. Willie Mays hit two and Orlando Cepeda, Tom Haller and rookie Jim Ray Hart belted one each. Marichal had four strike outs in the complete game effort. The crowd at Candlestick Park was the largest at that time to ever watch a league game.

1965 at Pittsburgh

Marichal went on the road and was locked in a fierce pitchers' duel with the Pirates' Bob Veale. Although he pitched a brilliant game, he was the victim of hard luck. Bob Bailey hit a home run leading off the tenth inning for the 1-0 Pittsburgh win. Marichal pitched a complete game loss and struck out nine batters. Bailey's shot was only the fifth hit that Marichal allowed on the day. Until the game-winning blast, Marichal had not allowed a runner past second base.

1966 vs. Chicago (N)

Marichal was dominant as ever in this contest. He had a perfect game going into the seventh inning as he and the Giants whipped the Cubs

9-1. He allowed only three hits total in the game. Marichal retired the first 18 men to face him. Then, center fielder Ty Cline reach safely on an error to open the seventh inning. Second baseman Glenn Beckert then slammed a double for the first Chicago hit. Cline scored on Billy Williams' infield out. It was Marichal's fourth consecutive complete game on Opening Day.

1967 at St. Louis

Marichal was matched-up against the great Bob Gibson. The fiery Cardinal ace was always known for his fierce competitive nature. During the game, the two traded insults in an ongoing shouting match. Gibson claimed that Marichal tried to hit him. Later in the game, the two collided when Gibson hit a slow roller to Marichal and he tried to tag him. Marichal allowed 14 hits and six runs over seven innings, taking only his second (and final) Opening Day loss of his career. Gibson shutdown the Giants' bats, allowing just five singles. The only bright spot for the Giants was young centerfielder Ken Henderson who was 3-for-4 in the leadoff spot.

1968 vs. New York (N)

Marichal was not involved in the decision in this game, where the Giants had to overcome a 4-1 deficit to the New York Mets. San Francisco scored three runs in the bottom of the ninth inning, including the winning tally on an errant relay throw for the victory. Marichal allowed four runs over the first three innings, all the result of Ron Swoboda's bat. The future World Series hero hit a run-scoring single in the first inning and then hit a three-run bomb in the third inning. Marichal struck out three and did not allow a walk. Frank Linzy earned the win.

1969 at Atlanta

For the second consecutive season, Juan Marichal did not earn a decision in this opener and reliever Fran Linzy did. However, the result was just the opposite as the Braves rallied for the win in this one. Marichal allowed three runs, six hits and two walks over six innings. He also struck out three batters.

1971 at San Diego

Marichal was back on track for this opener in San Diego. He pitched a five-hit shutout against the struggling Padres. Marichal walked one, struck out eight and allowed only one runner as far as second base. Willie Mays supplied the power with his 629th career home run before the record San Diego Stadium crowd.

1972 at Houston

Like a broken record, Marichal struck again with a shutout win on Opening Day. However, this one was not his usual complete game. Marichal kept the Astros in check allowing just six hits and striking out seven before being removed for a pinch-hitter in the ninth inning. He and Don Wilson dueled for five innings until the Giants tallied two on their way to a 5-0 win.

1973 at Cincinnati

In his last Opening Day start for the Giants, Marichal threw a complete game, 4-1 victory over Cincinnati. Marichal halted the mighty bats of the Big Red Machine who were defending National League champions. Over nine innings he scattered seven Red hits in the windy and chilly 40-degree weather at Riverfront Stadium. Marichal had trailed 1-0 after two innings, but Bobby Bonds and Chris Speier each delivered run-scoring hits in the rally.

07/31/71: Dave Kingman's Memorable 2nd Major League Game vs. Pittsburgh

Dave Kingman, playing in just his second Major League game, wore out Pittsburgh Pirate pitching on this day. Kingman replaced Giants' starting first baseman Willie McCovey early in the game. In the fourth inning, he smashed a run-scoring double. In the seventh inning, Kingman cracked a grand slam home run off of ace reliever Dave Giusti to help San Francisco tally seven runs in the frame. The Giants won the slugfest 15-11.

1971: National League Western Division Champions

The Giants won the National League Western Division title for the first time since the league expansion to two divisions, in 1971. The team won the division by one game with a 90-72 record. Bobby Bonds led the team in many offensive categories. Bonds batted .288; hit 33 home runs and had 102 runs batted in. The pitching corps was led by Gaylord Perry's 280 innings and 2.76 earned-run average. Juan Marichal led the staff with 18 wins and four shutouts. Oddly, the Giant lineup boasted *no* .300 hitters or 20-game winners. This was the first time a championship team did so since 1876. This season marked the 14th consecutive winning season for the club, every year since the club moved from New York. The next several years would be lean and the club would struggle to keep from going below the .500 mark.

1971 National League Championship Series vs. Pittsburgh

"The Year of the Fox" was 1971 in San Francisco. Manager Charlie Fox guided the team to the National League Western Division title by one game over the Dodgers. The club was a unique blend of youngsters and veterans. In the National League Championship Series, the Giants faced the Pittsburgh Pirates, who they had defeated nine times in 12 regular season meetings. Gaylord Perry pitched the Giants to a 5-4 win in Game 1. However the Pirates' hitting and pitching was too strong and they dominated the next three games and slammed the door to win the series and the Pennant.

Gaylord Perry, Career

Often over-shadowed by the exploits of fellow teammate Juan Marichal, Gaylord Perry was every bit a great pitcher in his own right. Perry pitched for the Giants from 1962-71 and had a career record of 134-109 and an earned-run average of 2.96 with San Francisco. He went on to win over 300 games for his career. Perry's dominance really came to light in 1967 when he threw 40 consecutive scoreless innings and had four shutouts during that period. Unbelievably, he finished the season with a 15-17 record, having experienced an amazing 10 one-run losses during the campaign. While with the Giants, he was a workhorse amassing almost 2,300 innings. Perry is in the Top-10 of virtually every San Francisco pitching category. Perry played with San Francisco from 1962 through 1971. He was elected to the Baseball Hall-of-Fame in 1991.

01/15/72: Giants Part of First International Player Trade in Major League History

The Giants and Lotte Orions of Japan announced the first international player trade in Major League Baseball history in mid-January, 1972. Owner Horace Stoneham himself completed the deal in which San Francisco gave an unconditional release to Frank Johnson so he may play for the Orions. Likewise, the Orions released right-handed pitcher Toru Hamaura so he would sign with the Giants. In reality, the trade was no more than a publicity event to promote the three-game series between the two clubs in Honolulu, Hawaii a couple of months later in the "Friendship Series."

03/24-26/72: Giants Face Lotte Orions in "Friendship Series" in Honolulu, Hawaii

In a three-game exhibition set called the "Friendship Series," the Giants battled the Lotte Orions from Japan from March 24-26. The series observed the 20th anniversary of the official end of World War II between

Japan and the United States. Occupation forces officially departed from Japan in 1952. All games were played at the famed termite pit, Honolulu Stadium. The stadium was dubbed as such because it was an aging, all wood facility. The games between the two teams marked the third consecutive spring that the Giants competed against the Orions. In the Giants' 1970 tour of Japan, the clubs played four times. In 1971, the Orions closed-out their tour of the United States mainland with two games at the newly renovated Candlestick Park.

08/29/72: Jim Barr - Sets Consecutive Batters Retired Record (41 vs. Pittsburgh / St. Louis)

In 1972, young prospect Jim Barr achieved a unique place in baseball history with a record that is considered obscure today, even in the information era that boasts bushels of statistics that float around ballparks, periodicals and the Internet. Barr retired 41 consecutive batters, over two straight starts. That is 13 2/3 consecutive perfect innings, the equivalent to almost 1 1/2 perfect games. However, he did not pitch a full perfect game or even a no-hitter during this stretch. It started on August 23 when he faced the defending World Champion Pittsburgh Pirates at Candlestick Park. Barr pitched a masterful two-hit shutout and retired the final 21 batters (7.0 innings) he faced. Six days later on August 29, Barr's next start was in St. Louis. There, he set down the first 20 Cardinals he faced and continued the streak to 41 straight batters retired. The incredible streak ended with two out in the seventh inning when right fielder Bernie Carbo doubled to left field. Barr notched his second consecutive complete game shutout. His efforts broke the previous mark set by Harvey Haddix (38) in 1959.

Dave Rader: 1972 *Sporting News* National League Rookie of the Year

Catcher Dave Rader earned 1972 *Sporting News* National League Rookie of the Year honors. For the season, Rader was a workhorse and played in 133 games, batted .259, hit six home runs and drove in 41 as he replaced Dick Dietz behind the plate.

Marichal and Perry: 1960's Decade Second Best One-Two Pitching Combo in Major League Baseball

Juan Marichal and Gaylord Perry were an overwhelming and dominant pitching duo for the Giants' staff during the 1960s. Both emerged as premier right-handers that baffled and at times completely shut down opponents. As documented, Marichal holds the mark for wins by a pitcher for the decade (191). Combined, Marichal and Perry (95) won a total of 286 games from 1960-69. This is second best for teammate tandems during that time span. The pair was narrowly edged-out by just nine wins by the Don Drysdale (158) and Sandy Koufax (137) combination from the rival Dodgers; they totaled 295 victories. Both marks easily out-rival any other team pitching combinations by a large margin.

Mays and McCovey: One of the Most Prolific Home Run Duos in History (2nd)

Just as Marichal and Perry provided a dominating one-two pitching punch, Willie Mays and Willie McCovey, who could smack the cover off the ball, joined together to form one of the mightiest home run duos of all time. Between 1959 and 1971, the two teamed up for an astounding 800 home runs together and terrorized National League pitching year after year. That is second best all-time for Major League Baseball and the National League, just short of the 863 of the Hank Aaron-Eddie Mathews duo of the Milwaukee / Atlanta Braves. Mays and McCovey finished ahead of the mighty Babe Ruth and Lou Gehrig of the famed "Murderer's Row" Yankee teams in the late 1920s and early 1930s. At the time, the two also owned the second best National League total for one season with 91 in 1965.

Willie Mays, Career

Considered by many experts and fans to be the best all-around baseball player of his era and perhaps in the entire history of the game. Willie was one of the first ballplayers to possess all of the key tools of the game: hitting, power, speed, fielding, and throwing. Mays played in 24 All-Star games. Willie had a lifetime batting average of .302 and 660 home runs. His home run total is good for fourth on the all-time list, behind only Hank Aaron, Babe Ruth and Barry Bonds. He was selected as the National League Rookie of the Year in 1951 and Most Valuable Player in 1954 and 1965. Mays was chosen as a member of the All-1960s, All-1970s, and All-Time San Francisco Giants Team in 1999. Also selected as the starting outfielder on Major League Baseball's All-Century Team. Mays was elected to the Baseball Hall-of-Fame in 1979. He played for San Francisco from 1958 to mid-1972. Willie continued to be involved with the Giants and the community after his retirement.

Willie Mays: Extra-Inning Home Runs Record

The mark of a true champion is his ability to perform well in the clutch, under pressure. Willie Mays consistently proved he was one of the best. Mays smashed an amazing 22 home runs in extra innings during his career. This figure put him ahead of all the other great sluggers of the game; Babe Ruth is the next closest challenger with 16. An important but often overlooked statistical fact, this record is not publicized nearly as much as many of Mays' other amazing feats.

04/12/73: Willie McCovey - Two Home Runs in One Inning vs. Houston

Willie McCovey became the eighth National League player to hit two home runs in one inning when he accomplished the feat against the Houston Astros. McCovey victimized pitchers Ken Forsch and Jim Crawford in the fourth inning, driving in four runs with the pair of long balls. McCovey's dual home runs in one frame were the first by a

National Leaguer since 1949, when another Giant (NY) Sid Gordon, achieved the feat.

05/01/73: One of the Greatest Comeback Wins in Major League History vs. Pittsburgh

The greatest come-from-behind victory in San Francisco Giants' history occurred when they defeated the Pittsburgh Pirates 8-7 in 1973. Not many of the paid crowd of 7,972 were left when the Giants came to bat in the bottom of the ninth trailing 7-1. Those who did stay saw one of the greatest ninth inning rallies in history. Pirates' starter Bob Moose walked the bases loaded to start the inning. Ramon Hernandez came on in relief and gave up a grand slam home run to pinch hitter Chris Arnold to make the score 7-5. Gary Matthews kept the rally alive with a double. Dave Rader and Jim Howarth each then walked, and the bases were loaded again. With Bobby Bonds coming up, the Pirates made another pitching change and brought in ace closer Dave Giusti. Bonds responded by hitting a bases-clearing double to give the Giants an incredible and unlikely 8-7 win.

07/24/73: Bobby Bonds All-Star Game Most Valuable Player

Bobby Bonds continued the Giant tradition in All-Star Games. Bobby earned Most Valuable Player honors by going 2-for-2, with a home run and a double, scored one run and drove in two. The National League won the game at Kansas City 7-1. A record 54 players were used in the game, including Willie Mays, who struck out in his final All-Star appearance. Fellow Giants' outfielder Bobby Bonds, in the midst of his finest overall season, entered the game during the fourth inning to replace starter Billy Williams. He then proceeded to smack a two-run home run in his first at-bat in the fifth inning off California's Bill Singer. He secured his Most Valuable Player Award in the seventh inning when he ran out a lazy single for a very exciting double with some audacious base running.

Gary Matthews: 1973 *Sporting News* National League Rookie of the Year

After a brief stint with the Giants in 1972, Gary Matthews won the starting left field job for the team in 1973. "Sarge" was one of the most exciting players to come along in a while. For the season, Matthews batted .300, hit 12 home runs and drove in 58. For his efforts, he was named the 1973 *Sporting News* National League Rookie of the Year. Matthews played five seasons in a San Francisco uniform.

Jim Ray Hart, Career

This was another Giant in the long line of sluggers developed in the minor-league system. During the years of 1964-68, Hart averaged nearly 28 home runs and 90 runs batted in per season. Teamed with Mays and McCovey, Jim Ray was a consistent provider of solid power in the Giants' lineup. Overall, Hart's career was severely affected by injuries that impacted his ability. In 1963, his first season, he incurred a broken shoulder blade (vs. Bob Gibson) and a concussion against the St. Louis Cardinals, on separate occasions. After 1968, he never appeared in more than 95 games in any season. Hart played with the Giants until he was traded in 1973.

Juan Marichal, Career

Arguably one of the foremost pitchers of his era. Marichal provided the pitching backbone for a well-rounded Giants' squad during the 1960s. He was selected to play in nine All-Star games and pitched a no-hitter in 1963. For his career, Marichal won 238 games for the Giants. Marichal is the leader in virtually every San Francisco pitching category. He was selected as a member of the All-1960s, All-1970s, and All-Time San Francisco Giant Team in 1999. Juan was a Giant from 1960 to 1973. He was elected to the Baseball Hall-of-Fame in 1983.

Chapter 6: The Lean Years and Rock Bottom (1974-1985)

09/03/74: John Montefusco's Memorable Major League Debut at Los Angeles

Rookie pitcher John Montefusco made one of the most notable debuts in Giants' history at Los Angeles. In early September, 1974, Ron Bryant took the mound at Dodger Stadium in a meaningless late-season game. Although spotted with a 2-0 lead, Bryant allowed Los Angeles to score four runs on just one hit, three walks, a passed ball and one error. With no outs in the bottom of the first inning, manager Wes Westrum summoned rookie right-hander John Montefusco in for long relief. Montefusco had just arrived at the stadium prior to the start of the game. After being called from the bullpen, Montefusco ignored the waiting golf cart and sprinted from the distant bullpen to the mound. Cool and collected, John squelched the Dodger rally in the inning, getting one out on a ground ball and the next two on strikeouts; he marched off the mound with both hands raised in victory. He would pitch the rest of the way, nine full innings, allowing just one more run and help the Giants to a 9-5 victory.

Even more exciting than a relief pitcher throwing nine innings, one of the longest in the modern era, Montefusco helped the Giants in more ways than with just his pitching. In the second inning, John strolled to the plate for his first Major League at-bat and earned a walk, and eventually scored, as part of a Giant comeback rally. In the third inning, Montefusco really made his mark and punctuated the night. With two outs and one runner on base, he smashed a Charlie Hough knuckleball over the right field wall into the bleachers. The Giants were able to hold on the rest of the way and defeat the Dodgers 9-5, with Montefusco earning the win.

Bobby Bonds, Career

Perhaps the most exciting young player to come along in more than a decade when he appeared on the scene in 1968, Bonds was one of the first players of his era to combine power and speed. Bonds routinely achieved the exclusive 30-30 level, once just missing the elusive 40-40 mark; Bonds ended the 1973 season with 39 home runs and 43 stolen bases. He stalled at 38 home runs for the last three weeks of the season, hitting his 39th on the last day of the campaign. Bonds ranks in the Top-10 in virtually every San Francisco offensive category. His impact on the game set the table for many players for the next two decades to come. Prior to Rickey Henderson, Bobby held the Major League record for lead-off home runs to start a game. Bonds still holds the National league record with 30. Bobby died at the young age of 57 in 2003.

John D'Acquisto: 1974 *Sporting News* National League Rookie of the Year

The Giants continued their fortune with the development of good young talent in the farm system into the mid '70s. John D'Acquisto provided strong pitching support for the team, starting 36 games. On the year, D'Acquisto had a 12-14 record with 3.77 earned-run average, five complete games and one shutout. For his efforts, he was named the 1974 *Sporting News* National League Rookie of the Year. This campaign was the best of D'Acquisto's career. He pitched five seasons for the Giants before being traded.

08/24/75: Ed Halicki No-Hitter vs. New York (N)

Right-handed pitcher Ed Halicki hurled a no-hitter against the New York Mets in the second game of a doubleheader at Candlestick Park. After the New York Mets won the first game 9-5 in San Francisco, Halicki recorded a controversial no-hitter in beating the Mets in the second game. The 6'7" right-hander struck out 10 Mets to improve his record to 8-10. The controversy arose when Rusty Staub hit a ball off Halicki's leg which caromed to second baseman Derrel Thomas. He picked the ball up to make a play and then dropped it. The official scorer Joe Sargis ruled it an E-4, sparking many to say he subscribed to the theory that the first hit in a no-hit game should be a "solid one." Halicki struck out 10 batters and stifled the Mets 6-0 before a crowd of 24,132.

John Montefusco: 1975 *Sporting News* National League Rookie of the Year

For the second year in a row, the Giants had a pitcher selected as Rookie of the Year. John Montefusco became part of the Giants starting rotation and answered with 15 wins. He also tossed four shutouts and 10 complete games and had a 2.88 earned-run average. "The Count", as he was known, was named the 1975 *Sporting News* National League Rookie of the Year. John remained with the Giants through the 1980 season. Although he made his Major League debut in late-1974, Montefusco was still considered a rookie, having pitched only 39 1/3 innings.

09/29/76: John Montefusco No-Hitter at Atlanta

John Montefusco pitched the first road no-hitter in San Francisco Giants' history at Atlanta. Montefusco stymied Brave hitters on just 97 pitches and struck out four in a 9-0 victory. Montefusco walked just one batter, Jerry Royster in the fourth inning, on a 3-1 count. Montefusco (16-14), "The Mouth that Roared," proclaimed in the locker room afterwards that, "The Count is back!" Gary Alexander caught the near perfect game. An interesting note to the performance is that amazingly 92 of the 97 pitches by Montefusco were fastballs. Shortstop Johnnie LeMaster provided the offense with a triple, double and three runs batted in.

Bob Lurie, Owner

Bob Lurie was viewed as a savior when he put together a last-minute deal to rescue the Giants from being sold to a Toronto brewery in 1976. San Francisco Mayor George Moscone received a temporary restraining order blocking the move and looked for a local buyer. Lurie had a wealthy San Francisco heritage and was on the Giants' Board of Directors. He partnered with Arizona cattleman Bud Herseth to pull the deal together and keep the Giants in San Francisco. Under Lurie's ownership, the club experienced resurgence after some very lean years in the mid-1970s. In the mid 1980s, the club was once again on the verge of being a serious contender. He hired Al Rosen as his general manager and Roger Craig as his field manager. The Giants responded with winning the National League Pennant in 1989. Lurie sold the club in 1993.

Larry Herndon: 1976 *Sporting News* National League Rookie of the Year

For the fifth consecutive year, a San Francisco Giant was awarded the *Sporting News* National League Rookie of the Year trophy. Larry Herndon played 110 games for the Giants in the outfield. He batted .288, hit two home runs, drove in 23 and stole 12 bases. Herndon played six seasons for the Giants.

05/08/77: Giants Hire the Great Karl Wallenda to Boost Sagging Attendance

In an effort to boost the lowest attendance in baseball, the Giants hired the great 72-year-old world famous tightrope acrobat Karl Wallenda to navigate a high wire stretched above the field. Between games of a Sunday double-header versus the New York Mets, Wallenda carefully negotiated the slim rope from the upper deck in left field to the upper deck in right field. The normally gusty winds seemed to cease for a time, in order for Wallenda to perform his 20-minute "walk in the park." Wallenda previously appeared at other ballparks, but none with the reputation of Candlestick Park. The Giants swept the double-header from the Mets, as game two was suspended in the seventh inning with San Francisco leading 10-0. Although the game was originally scheduled to be resumed the next time New York played in San Francisco that July, the game was not, and it appears in the books as it ended that day.

06/27/77: Willie McCovey - Two Home Runs in One Inning at Cincinnati

Willie McCovey became the only player in Major League history to hit two home runs in the same inning twice in a career. In the sixth inning at Cincinnati, McCovey hit the two shots off Jack Billingham and Joe Hoerner; the second one a grand slam home run. That grand slam was the 17th of his career, giving him the all-time National League record.

05/28/78: Mike Ivie Memorable Grand Slam Home Run vs. Los Angeles

Mike Ivie hit a career-high .308 for the Giants in 1978 when he backed up the aging Willie McCovey at first base. He showed little range, but was a useful pinch-hitter. Ivie went 12-for-31 (.387) in that role and tied a Major League record with two pinch-hit grand slam home runs that season. One of those blasts by Ivie was one of the most memorable home runs in Giants' history, against the hated Los Angeles Dodgers. Ivie appeared as a pinch hitter in the sixth inning and thrilled the crowd of 57,475 with a grand slam off Don Sutton. The hit powered the Giants to a 6-5 win. This was voted the favorite 1970s Memory by fans in a website ballot vote in 2003.

06/30/78: Willie McCovey's 500th Career Home Run at Atlanta

In the first game of a 10-9, 10-5 doubleheader sweep by the Braves, Willie McCovey smashed his 500th career home run. On a 0-2 pitch from Atlanta's Jamie Easterly, Willie launched his 500th over the left field fence at Fulton County Stadium. McCovey became the 12th member of the 500 Home Run Club and was on his way to breaking the National League mark for home runs by a left-handed batter. McCovey broke former Giant Mel Ott's mark of 511. His 521 career home runs tied him with boyhood hero Ted Williams and were bested by another Giant left-hander, Barry Bonds.

Charles "Chub" Feeney, General Manager

Three years before his birth, Feeney's grandfather Charles Stoneham paid $1 million to buy the New York Giants baseball club. When he returned from World War II in 1946, his uncle Horace Stoneham was in control of the Giants, and Charles, who earned the nickname Chub when he was a baby, was offered a minor front office job.

Chub worked part time for the Giants while attending Fordham Law School. In 1950 he was promoted to the position of Vice President, effectively becoming the club's general manager. The Giants won the Pennant in 1951, and won a World Championship in 1954. In 1957, Horace Stoneham announced he was moving the franchise to San Francisco. Chub was reluctant to follow his uncle at first, but he immediately became enchanted with the city upon moving there. The Giants captured the National League Pennant again in 1962. In 1969 Feeney was in line to be named Commissioner of Baseball, but a number of American League owners objected, and Bowie Kuhn was chosen instead. One year after losing out on a chance to be commissioner, Chub Feeney would unanimously be selected to fill the office of the retiring National League President Warren Giles. Chub Feeney would hold the office for 16 years. Feeney, a firm traditionalist, regarded protecting the league from the designated hitter as his greatest achievement in office. After stepping down, Feeney took a job as President of the San Diego Padres, but would step down after just 15 months on the job, as the team was going through a change in ownership.

Feeney spent 22 years in the Giants' organization, mostly as general manager. Feeney diligently worked to make the franchise a superior organization. He completed many successful trades and developed the Giants' minor-league system to be one of the best during the '50s and '60s.

04/10/79: John Tamargo Game Winning Home Run vs. San Diego (Opening Day)

On Opening Day 1979, the Giants entered the bottom of the ninth inning tied 2-2 with the San Diego Padres. Reserve catcher John Tamargo came off the bench to hit a two-out pinch-hit home run off John D'Acquisto to spark a 4-2 Giant win. Willie McCovey had reached base just ahead of Tamargo with a pinch-hit single off of ex-Giant D'Acquisto. Vida Blue received credit for the win before a spirited crowd of 57,484. Tamargo hit four home runs during his entire 135 game career.

09/06/79: Rob Andrews' Two Home Runs in One Game vs. Seaver (Three For Entire Career)

In a late-season game at Cincinnati's Riverfront Stadium, the Giants faced the Reds. Not known for his power, light-hitting second baseman Rob Andrews batted second in the lineup behind leadoff hitter Max Venable. His job was to get on base in front of the power hitters in the middle of the order. The Giants were facing one of the best pitchers of the era, Tom Seaver. On this day, Andrews experienced the magic that many players dream of in the third and fifth innings. Amazingly, he belted two home runs versus the fireballing ace. Seaver shut down the rest of the team, though, scattering just five hits en route to a 12-3 Reds' victory. During his career, in nearly 1,500 at-bats, Andrews swatted just three total home runs.

07/06/80: Willie McCovey Final Major League At-Bat / RBI at Los Angeles

A truly remarkable career came to an end on July 6, 1980. In his last Major League at-bat, at Dodger Stadium in Los Angeles, "Stretch" produced one last hurrah. Willie McCovey concluded his great career by driving in a crucial run against the Dodgers at Los Angeles in his final at-bat. Pinch-hitting, he lifted a run-scoring sacrifice fly in the eight inning off Rick Sutcliffe to score Jack Clark from third base and give the Giants a 4-3 lead. The Giants went on to win the game 7-4 in 10 innings. After the game, McCovey was placed on the Voluntary Retired List.

10/03/80: Triple Play Turned by Three Giants' Rookies

On this day, a real baseball rarity occurred. The triple play in baseball is a rare enough event. To have three true rookie players involved in each aspect of the play is even more significantly remote, but it happened.

Late into the season, three Giants' rookies completed the feat on October 3, 1980. In the fourth inning, San Diego's Dave Cash hit a line drive to second baseman Guy Sularz who threw to shortstop Joe Pettini covering second base. Pettini then threw to first baseman Rich Murray for the third out. It was the first triple play in the nearly 20-year history of Candlestick Park. Native San Franciscian Fred Breining was the pitcher. The play was not inspiring at all to the team, as they were trounced by the Padres 12-0.

Willie McCovey, Career

Considered by many to be the most popular San Francisco Giant of all-time, Willie spent 19 years with the Giants' organization as a player in two stints. McCovey is the leader or runner-up in virtually every San Francisco offensive category and holds many franchise records. "Stretch" holds the all-time National League record for career grand slam home runs with 18. His 521 home runs place him in the top 15 on the all-time list. He was selected as a member of the All-1960s, All-1970s, and All-Time San Francisco Giant Team in 1999. McCovey was elected to the baseball Hall-of-Fame in 1986. His nickname, "Stretch", was given to him due to his superb fielding ability, specifically when reaching for poorly thrown balls off the first base bag yet stretching, scooping and holding them. In retirement, Big Mac continued to work for the Giants, representing them in community affairs.

08/09/81: Vida Blue First Game-Winning Pitcher in All-Star Game for Both Leagues

Vida became the first pitcher to win an All-Star game for both leagues while pitching a perfect inning of relief at Cleveland. The tight 5-4 National League victory was highlighted by the highest attendance and most players ever used in an All-Star game, as well. Blue was also the winning pitcher for the American League in 1971 at Detroit as a member of the Oakland Athletics. Vida also held the distinction of being the first hurler to start an All-Star game for each league when he appeared for the Giants in the 1978 contest.

"Willie Mac" Award Throughout the Years (1980 -)

In 1980, shortly after his retirement, the Giants established the Willie Mac Award in honor of the great slugger Willie McCovey. This is presented annually to the Giant player who best exemplifies the inspiration, spirit and leadership displayed by McCovey during his career. Some of the winners include: Joe Morgan, Mike Krukow, Dave Dravecky, and Robby Thompson. Krukow is the only two-time winner in history. The honor is awarded as the result of a player-only vote.

Willie McCovey: National League Career Grand Slam Home Run Record (18)

Willie McCovey was the most feared hitter of his generation. McCovey always seemed to come to the plate in crucial situations. Everyone knew that Willie had power in the clutch, especially when the bases were loaded. During his career, McCovey smashed 18 grand slam home runs, a National League record. Many of these are memorable. His total is also good enough for third on the all-time Major League list behind fellow Hall-of-Famers Lou Gehrig (23) and Eddie Murray (19).

Willie McCovey: Pinch-Hit Home Runs and Pinch-Hit Grand Slam Home Runs

Proving that he was a slugger in the clutch, McCovey was often used in late innings as a pinch-hitter, on off-days where he did not make an appearance in the field. McCovey responded by connecting for 51 hits off the bench, including cracking 16 pinch-hit home runs in his career. This figure is third on the all-time Major League list. Three of those pinch home runs were grand slams. This places him in a tie for first on the all-time list.

10/03/82: Joe Morgan Dramatic Home Run on Final Day of Season vs. Los Angeles

The Giants and Dodgers have one of the most emotional rivalries in all of professional sports. On the last day of the 1982 season, the Los Angeles Dodgers were battling the Atlanta Braves for the National League Western Division title. On October 3, 1982, 47,457 people came to Candlestick Park for a sole purpose. They wanted to see blue Los Angeles Dodger blood spilled on the turf. Giants' second baseman Joe Morgan responded and lined a three-run home run off Dodgers reliever Terry Forster with two on and two out in the seventh inning. The blast landed onto the facing of the football seats in right field. The blow powered a 5-3 Giants' victory that knocked the Dodgers out of the playoff race and handed the Division title to the Braves by one game. It was sweet revenge for the Giants, whom the Dodgers eliminated the day before with a 15-4 thrashing. A three-way divisional race came down to the last weekend, and the Dodgers and Giants inflicted fatal blows to one another on successive afternoons to let the third party slide into the playoffs. Nonetheless, Morgan's home run is still one of the greatest moments in Candlestick Park history because of the hurt it put on the hated Dodgers.

Frank Robinson, Manager

Success during Frank Robinson's managerial career did not come close to that of his playing career. However, he will always be remembered as a pioneer. Robinson holds the distinction of being the first African-American manager in both the American League (1975) and National League (1981). "Robby" guided the Giants' to back-to-back winning seasons in 1981 and 1982. In 1982, he was named the UPI Manager of the Year. He ended with a career record of 264-277 (.488) with the

Giants. He later managed the Expos and Nationals for several more seasons.

Bay Bridge Series vs. Oakland Athletics: A Post Spring Training Tradition

Commencing in 1983 and lasting thorough the 1998 season, the Giants and Oakland Athletics met annually in what was known as the "Bay Bridge Series." The series took place after the teams broke Spring Training camp in Arizona and returned to the Bay Area, prior to start of their respective regular seasons. The series originally started out as a two-game set for several years, with each team hosting one home game. If the teams split the two games, then the winner was determined by a home run hitting contest. In the latter years, the series was stretched to three games. The series was discontinued for the 1999 and 2000 seasons. The series resumed again in 2001 and continues each March.

Badge of Courage: *Croix* de Candlestick Program

The memorable *Croix* de Candlestick Program was the brainchild of a young marketing director named Larry Baer in 1983. Fans had long complained about the extreme frigid conditions endured while watching night games at Candlestick Park, and this was in the summer. Playing upon this, Baer developed the *Croix* de Candlestick pin as a symbol for the brave fans that stayed until the end of the extra-inning night games. Giants' pitcher Mike Krukow even wore one on his hat during that 1983 campaign. The club kept this custom until they left Candlestick Park in 1999. Baer went on to play a major role in the development and building of Pacific Bell Park and as a front office leader.

Crazy Crab: Reviled Giants' Mascot (Anti-Mascot)

The city of San Francisco has always been synonymous with great seafood and fish, especially crab, caught right beyond the Golden Gate. In 1984, the Giants introduced a new (their first) mascot, named Crazy Crab. Crazy Crab was marketed as a satire of prevailing mascots in professional sports at the time. The vast majority of Giants' fans said they did not want a mascot at all. Team officials introduced him with the twist of being an "anti-mascot" and fans were encouraged to boo and hiss at him. Crazy Crab was a pudgy, puffed and immobile creature that resembled a hamburger. Unfortunately the Giants were having a horrid season and were seated in dead last place. The poor Crab became the object of more hatred and abuse than was ever foreseen; he was battered by the fans, relentlessly pelted with food and beverage and even accosted by players who got into the act by dumping drinks and other things into the suit. He would trot out once per game specifically to be booed and pelted with peanut shells. The typically small crowds of the time obliged whole-heartedly. The '70s may have brought us bell bottoms and disco, but they also saw the beginnings of the mascot craze in professional sports.

As stated, the idea was to poke fun at traditional mascots. Television commercials depicted manager Frank Robinson having to be restrained from attacking the poor crustacean. The poor guy inside the suit was portrayed by actor Wayne Doba. The prodding worked all too well. With a 96-loss season soothing no souls, Crazy Crab became the extreme object of hatred and abuse. Broadcasters Mike Krukow and Duane Kuiper, both players during the year, indicated that they too used to provide abuse, drilling him with the rosin bag daily. Reserve catcher Steve Nicosia once donned the suit while he trashed the volatile Jeffrey Leonard's locker. While playing the Crab, Doba was even tackled by a San Diego Padres player and ended up filing a lawsuit against the team for back injuries. On the final day of the 1984 season, as he stood on the field in the suit before the game, Doba reportedly told a Giants executive, "I hope there's nobody up there with a gun." The nightmare for the bug-eyed object of foam derision ended after just one season. The Giants would not attempt another mascot, "anti" or real, again until 1997, when Lou Seal made his cautious debut. But no mascot will likely ever again as sharply define the term "love-hate" as the vaunted Crazy Crab. The Crab made one last appearance, smelly suit and all, being resuscitated for the last game at Candlestick Park on September 30, 1999. Fans were much kinder to the Crab this time around.

1984 All-Star Game at Candlestick Park

Neither league showed much offense in this edition of the All-Star Game that was considered a yawner. The National League finally triumphed 3-1. The highlight of the game was 19-year-old pitcher Dwight Gooden of the New York Mets. Gooden was masterful as he tied Carl Hubbel's record of striking out six consecutive batters in the game. Gary Cater was named the Most Valuable Player as he went 1-for-2, including a second inning home run off AL starter Dave Stieb.

Gary Lavelle, Career

Gary Lavelle was a cornerstone for the San Francisco bullpen for a full decade. Lavelle holds the San Francisco record for pitching appearances at 647. Lavelle won 10 games in a season on three occasions and posted an earned-run average under 3.00 eight times. His 127 career saves ranks third all-time for San Francisco. Gary played 11 seasons for San Francisco, through 1984.

Jack Clark, Career

Jack "The Ripper" Clark was one of the most feared hitters during his National League career. Clark posted solid power numbers, including career highs in home runs (27) and runs batted in (103) for the Giants in 1982. Clark also set the San Francisco consecutive game hitting streak record of 26 in 1978. He was selected as a member of the All-1970s San Francisco Giant Team in 1999. Clark played 10 seasons for the Giants.

The Quest for a New Ballpark, Part One - Political Defeats

After a very short period of time, it was apparent that Candlestick Park was not a very comfortable place to watch a game, day or night. Since the mid-1960s there had been talk of building a new stadium for the Giants. During his tenure as owner, Bob Lurie tried on several occasions to get voter approval in many different Bay Area communities for approval to build a new stadium. This included four defeats in the city of San Francisco alone. This led Lurie to finally sell the team to new ownership. The lack of a good venue also significantly limited the team in attracting free agent players, as they knew of the negative impact the park could have on their careers.

Chapter 7: Rebuilding and a New Beginning (1986-1989)

04/08/86: Will Clark First Major League At-Bat / Home Run vs. Nolan Ryan at Houston

Rookie first baseman Will Clark "thrilled" the crowd with a sizzling Major League debut as he hit a home run in his first at-bat against the legendary Nolan Ryan at the Houston Astrodome. Clark stroked a 1-1 pitch over the centerfield wall and the Giants went on to an 8-3 opening night victory over the Astros. Clark's initial brilliance continued for many seasons as he was one of the most clutch performers in the game for several years. The Astrodome had always been a very difficult place to play for the Giants and was well-known for not being a hitter friendly park. For the first part of the season, manager Roger Craig had inserted Clark in the number two hole in the line up, not knowing much about his bat control and power, which could help the club in another spot.

09/14/86: Bob Brenly Memorable Game vs. Atlanta (Errors / Heroics)

Bob Brenly, the Giants' catcher, was inserted into the lineup as a sub at third base in this late season game by manager Roger Craig. The day turned out to be one of the most bittersweet for any Major League player in history. In the fourth inning, Brenly tied a nearly century-old Major League record by committing four errors in one inning versus the Atlanta Braves. Brenly, whose normal position was catcher, atoned for his errors by mounting offensive comebacks throughout the game. He did this by hitting a home run in the fifth inning, smashing a game-tying two-run single in the seventh inning and belting a two-out game-winning home run in the ninth inning. The Giants won 7-6.

Mike Krukow: 20 Game Winner in 1986

Mike Krukow was acquired as part of the Joe Morgan trade from Philadelphia in 1983. Krukow provided strong starting pitching support during the 1980s. In 1986, he achieved a career high 20 wins (20-9, 3.05 earned run average). His 20th win came on the final day of the 1986 season at Dodger Stadium. Starting on just three days rest, Mike pitched 6 1/3 innings, struck out four and walked one in an 11-2 laugher. He was the first 20 game winner for the Giants since 1973 and the first right-hander to reach 20 since 1970. The win allowed the Giants to finish ahead of the Dodgers for the first time since 1971. Krukow went on to be one of the most popular baseball analysts in the Bay Area, paired with former teammate Duane Kuiper.

Robby Thompson: 1986 *Sporting News* National League Rookie of the Year

During Spring Training in 1986, Robby Thompson earned a spot as the starting second baseman for the Giants. In his short professional career, Thompson never even played at the Triple-A level. Thompson batted .271, hit seven home runs and drove in 47 runs for the season. He also led the team with 149 hits, 73 runs scored and eighteen sacrifices. Thompson was named 1986 *Sporting News* National League Rookie of the Year. Thompson had a solid career wearing only a San Francisco uniform. Robby retired after the conclusion of the 1996 season.

Baseball Rarity: Home Runs by San Francisco Giants' Relief Pitchers

Many fans realize that for a pitcher to hit a home run is somewhat rare. Once, the game witnessed numerous pitchers that were solid threats at the plate and could muscle up and hit the ball over the fence. These players gave managers an additional weapon, sometimes using a good hitting pitcher as a pinch hitter on an off-day. It was rare, but in games that went beyond 15 innings or so, managers had to get real creative. With this, for a relief pitcher to hit a home run is really a scarce event. Specific statistics chronicling this event are very hard to come by. Record books and statistical organizations do not maintain lists of such occurrences. Throughout the history of baseball, it has occurred periodically. It most cases, there is a certain amount of drama or importance attached, due to the nature of the situation. San Francisco Giants' relievers have by far hit more than any other club. Below are the details of each home run. Four of the home runs were hit at Candlestick Park, in 1965 by Frank Linzy, in 1966 and 1969 by Ray Sadecki and in 1999 by Felix Rodriguez. There is one very interesting note about the game in which Sadecki hit his home run. The 1966 contest in which Sadecki hit his blast witnessed another pitcher, Tony Cloninger of the Braves, have a record-breaking game, as he hit two grand slam home runs to set a mark for all batters. Until 1999 he was the only player in the entire history of the National League to ever do so.

Game Date	Giant's Pitcher	Opposing Team & Pitcher
07/28/65	Frank Linzy	St. Louis Cardinals Ray Washburn
07/03/66	Ray Sadecki	Atlanta Braves Tony Cloninger
04/15/69	Mike McCormick	Cincinnati Reds Wayne Granger
05/28/69	Ray Sadecki	Chicago Cubs Ken Holtzman
09/03/74	John Montefusco	Los Angeles Dodgers Charlie Hough
09/28/74	Ed Halicki	Cincinnati Reds Fred Norman
08/22/80	Tom Griffin	Philadelphia Phillies Steve Carlton
09/27/83	Greg Minton	Atlanta Braves Gene Garber
09/05/86	Scott Garrelts	Montreal Expos Bert Roberge
09/28/87	Don Robinson	San Diego Padres Lance McCullers
04/10/99	Felix Rodriguez	San Diego Padres Andy Ashby

Vida Blue, Career

Vida is considered one of the most popular athletes to ever play in the Bay Area. Vida came to the Giants in the biggest blockbuster trade in team history in late March, 1978. Immediately, he had an impact and helped resurrect the team into contention for the division flag. Blue added strength to a young club with his 18-10 record and 2.79 earned-run average. Blue possessed an overpowering fastball that baffled hitters in both leagues for years. Blue ended his Giant career with a 72-58 record, 3.52 earned-run average, over 1,000 innings pitched and seven shutouts. He was selected as a member of the All-1970s San

Francisco Giant Team in 1999. Blue spent six seasons with the Giants during his two stints with the club. For years, Vida has worked for the Giants in various public relations capacities, his most popular being Commissioner of the Junior Giants community baseball program.

1987: National League Western Division Champions

San Francisco won their first division title in 15 years in 1987. Just two years after losing 100 games, the Giants won the race with a 90-72 record. Will Clark led the attack with a .308 batting average, 35 home runs and 91 runs batted in. Journeyman Mike LaCoss led the pitching staff with 13 wins. The success was primarily due to the efforts of Roger Craig and Al Rosen.

1987 National League Championship Series vs. St. Louis

In the National League Championship Series, the Giants battled the St. Louis Cardinals. In a series that had several memorable games, the Giants took a 3-2 series lead going back to St. Louis looking for the fourth win to vault them into the World Series. Game 6 proved to be pivotal. The Giants received a great pitching performance from Dave Dravecky but fell 1-0, forcing a decisive Game 7. Game 7 turned out to be a major disappointment for the Giants as it proved to be all Cardinals. The Giants failed to score for the second consecutive day and lost 6-0. Jeffrey Leonard was named the series Most Valuable Player, a rarity for a player from a losing team.

Jeffrey Leonard: 1987 National League Championship Series Most Valuable Player (Losing Team)

Jeffrey Leonard became only the third player in postseason history to win the Most Valuable Player Award while his team lost the series. The rare and hollow honor was little consolation for Leonard and the Giants.

The Cardinals defeated the Giants four games to three and earned a spot in the World Series. Leonard hit home runs in each of the first four games of the series, taunting the Cardinals and their fans with his slow, deliberate "one-flap-down" trot, with one arm held against his side and the other arm extended, while he circled the bases. His final line for the series: .417 batting average, four home runs, five runs batted in, three walks and a .917 slugging percentage.

Al Rosen, General Manager

Part of Bob Lurie's new management regime of the mid-1980s was the hiring of general manager Al Rosen. A lifetime baseball man and former player with the Cleveland Indians, Rosen was recognized as a great executive of the game. Rosen made several key trades that brought the Giants two division crowns and a Pennant in a three-year period. Heads were spinning in baseball circles over Rosen's amazing overhaul of the Giants since he took command on September 18, 1985. A top-to-bottom shakeup of the Giants' baseball operations and a restoration of pride throughout the organization lifted San Francisco from a 100-loss club in 1985 to a third place finish in 1986 with an 83-79 mark. In 1987, during one remarkable span of just 49 days that began on Independence Day, Rosen executed three major transactions that catapulted the Giants to the top of the Western Division for keeps. The acquisitions of veteran pitchers Dave Dravecky, Craig Lefferts, Don Robinson and Rick Reuschel, plus young third baseman Kevin Mitchell, served notice on the other contenders that Rosen was playing hardball.

Chili Davis: Power from Both Sides of the Plate

Chili Davis was always a fan favorite while playing with the Giants for seven seasons. Davis was a home grown prospect who was a strong switch hitter that could hit for average and power. Davis smashed 101 home runs in his six full seasons with San Francisco. Davis ended his career with the third most home runs by a switch hitter in baseball history, behind only Mickey Mantle and Eddie Murray.

Greg Minton, Career

Greg Minton's career cemented himself as one of the best relief pitchers in San Francisco history. The "Moon Man" played for the Giants from 1975-1987. Minton totaled 125 saves for the Giants, fourth best all-time in the Giants' record book. He also holds the Major League record for consecutive innings pitched while not allowing a home run. For almost four years (1978-1982) and 269 innings opposing batters did not go deep on Minton. Greg was part of the organization for 13 seasons.

07/09/88: Ernest Riles - 10,000th Home Run in Giants' Franchise History vs. St. Louis

Reserve infielder Ernest Riles clubbed the 10,000th home run in Giant franchise history in a wild, wild game against the St. Louis Cardinals. Entering the game as a pinch-hitter, Riles clubbed the first pitch for a home run off Steve Peters in the seventh inning. Riles clout was part of one of the most powerful offensive explosions in team history, as the Giants won 21-2 at Candlestick Park. It was the same game that Chris Speier hit for the cycle, including two home runs.

08/10/89: Dave Dravecky - Dramatic Comeback from Cancer vs. Cincinnati

Although he only appeared in 27 games and won just 11 in his career as a Giant, Dave Dravecky will always be remembered as a Giant among Giants. After a bout with cancer and the removal of a malignant tumor and part of his muscle from his left (throwing) arm in late 1987, Dravecky fought back to pitch again less than a year later. His comeback reached a peak when he appeared again to beat the Cincinnati Reds 4-3 before an emotional crowd of 34,810 on August 10, 1989 at Candlestick Park. Dravecky's career finally ended five days later in Montreal when his arm snapped due to the resurgence of cancer. Ironically, Dravecky was the winning pitcher in that game. His 2-0 record for the year was significant and helped the Giants win the Western Division. In another dose of dark fate, Dravecky broke the arm again during the Giants' Pennant-winning celebration after defeating the Cubs. Ultimately, he would lose the arm to amputation. His courage and strength will always be remembered as an inspiration to all.

1989: National League Western Division and National League Champions

For the second time in three seasons, the Giants won the National League Western Division crown (92-72 record). Kevin Mitchell flourished and won National League Most Valuable Player honors, while supported by Will Clark and Matt Williams. Mitchell drilled 47 home runs and had 125 runs batted in. Rick Reuschel led the team with 17 wins, while Scott Garrelts had a 14-5 record and league-leading 2.28 earned-run average.

1989 National League Championship Series vs. Chicago (N)

The Giants' wait was over as they won their first National Pennant in 27 years. The Giants split the first two games with the Cubs in Chicago and then came back to San Francisco to dominate and take the next three games and earn a trip to the World Series. Kevin Mitchell and Series Most Valuable Player Will Clark led the Giants' attack.

10/09/89: Will Clark Powers the Giants Past the Cubs, into the World Series

On this day, the Giants won their first National League pennant since 1962 by defeating the Cubs 3-2 in Game 5 of the National League Championship Series. Slugger Will Clark batted a sizzling .650 in the series with eight runs batted in to win Most Valuable Player honors. In the bottom of the eighth inning, with the score tied 1-1 and starter Mike Bielecki having issued three straight two-out walks to load the bases, Chicago summoned the "Wild Thing," Mitch Williams, who quickly jumped ahead of Will Clark 0-2. After fouling off two fastballs, "The Thrill" lined a third heater back up the middle for a two-run single and a trip to the Fall Classic. It was the most dramatic moment of the series. This was voted the favorite 1980s Memory by fans in a website ballot vote in 2003.

Will Clark: 1989 National League Championship Series Most Valuable Player

Will Clark earned the Most Valuable Player award for his efforts against the Chicago Cubs in the 1989 National League Championship Series. Clark lined the game-winning hit to center field to drive in two runs in the seventh inning of Game 5. Clark's efforts propelled the Giants to their first World Series appearance since 1962. He ended the series with a .650 batting average, 24 total bases, 13 hits, eight runs, two home runs, and eight runs batted in.

10/17/89: Earthquake!

After losing the first two games of the 1989 World Series to Bay rival Oakland, Giants' fans were eagerly looking toward the team's chances at home in Game 3. On that calm Fall Tuesday, the entire world was watching and fans at Candlestick Park were waiting for the start of the game to begin. At precisely 5:04 p.m., a massive earthquake struck the Bay Area (Loma Prieta fault line). This was just a half hour before the scheduled start and the game. The jolt registered 7.1 on the Richter Scale. All electrical power was lost and the game was postponed for some 10 days as Bay Area residents recovered and got back in the swing of their lives. Surprisingly, old Candlestick Park incurred only minor damage and no fans were injured, but major damage was experienced to the surrounding areas. In all, the quake killed 67 people and caused $7 billion in damage. This still marks the only time in World Series history that a game was postponed for anything other than rain.

1989 World Series vs. Oakland

The Giants made their first World Series appearance since 1962. The opponent was their Bay Area rivals, the Oakland Athletics. The affair was dubbed the "Bay Bridge Series." Oakland broke out quick with two lop-sided victories at the Oakland Coliseum. The teams returned to Candlestick Park two days later but the series was halted for another 10 days due to the Loma Prieta earthquake. When play resumed, the Oakland hitting and pitching attacks were too much for the Giants and the A's won the series in four straight.

09/30/90: "I Now Pronounce You Husband and Wife:" Vida Gets Married at the 'Stick

Candlestick Park is noted for many "firsts" in the history of baseball and other endeavors, but in 1990 a truly unique event occurred. In a special but unusual ceremony, former Giants' pitcher Vida Blue married his fiancée Peggy Shannon on the pitcher's mound at Candlestick Park on September 30, 1990. The nuptial ceremony was conducted before a nice intimate crowd of 50,000 on Fan Appreciation Day. After being elegantly carted to the mound in a horse-drawn carriage, the bride was given away by Orlando Cepeda. The best man was none other than Willie McCovey.

Chris Speier, Career

Known as the "Alameda Rifle" for his strong throwing arm, Bay Area native Chris Speier burst onto the scene in 1971 and took over as the starting shortstop for a Giant team that went on to win the Western Division title. Speier provided stability at a key infield position and led the team in games played. Chris possessed a solid glove, strong arm, excellent defensive range and, at times, had pop in his bat. He combined with Tito Fuentes for several seasons to form a durable and effective double play combination. After a 10-year absence, Speier returned to be a strong role player off the bench for the 1987 and 1989 division championship teams. Speier played a total of 1,114 games for the Giants and was a two-time All-Star selection. Chris went on to a successful coaching career for several clubs.

Kevin Mitchell: 1989 National League Most Valuable Player

The 1989 season was memorable for the Giants' team. It was also one of the most memorable seasons for an individual player, Kevin Mitchell, as well. Mitchell earned National League Most Valuable Player honors with his .635 slugging percentage, 47 home runs and 125 runs batted in. He was the first San Francisco player to earn the Most Valuable Player since Willie McCovey in 1969. Mitchell provided significant pop in the lineup during his four-plus seasons with the Giants.

Roger Craig, Manager

Manager Roger Craig will always be remembered for his success in turning around a Giant team that lost 100 games in 1985 and then making them into division champions within two years. Craig, the "Humm Baby" teamed with general manager Al Rosen to bring respect from the baseball world back to San Francisco. Before his retirement, Craig led the Giants to two National League Western Division crowns and one National League Pennant. He ended with a career record 586-566 (.509) with the Giants. Perhaps his most significant contribution was teaching the young pitching staff how to throw the split-finger fastball.

Thompson - Uribe Double Play Combination

The Giants have had several infielders that have exhibited mastery with the leather. The double play combination of Jose Uribe (shortstop) and Robby Thompson (second base) absolutely sizzled around the bag and provided the cornerstone of a solid defensive infield in the late '80s and early '90s. The combo worked their magic together from 1986 through 1992. The entire infield of Uribe, Thompson, Williams and Clark was one of the best in the National League during that span.

Giants Fantasy Camp

The Giants' franchise was one of the first to offer their fans the opportunity to "play like a pro." Also known as "Fantasy Camp," it allows regular fans (30 years of age or older) to come and experience a whole week of real baseball like a professional. It mirrors a week of Spring Training in Arizona. Campers are issued full uniforms, kept healthy by team training personnel, placed on teams and play full games on the actual field the Giants use for their Spring Training activities.

The camp is staffed by many favorite all-time San Francisco Giants' players and coaches. They teach clinics for the attendees to learn the basics for all key aspects of the game, including hitting, fielding, throwing, pitching and base running. Fans also experience "bull sessions" and "kangaroo court," just like the guys in the Big Leagues. The camp has been run for many years by ex-Giant second baseman Rob Andrews and staffed by such former professionals as: Vida Blue, Rich Murray, Max Venable, Gary Matthews, Mark Grant, Bill Laskey, Gary Lavelle, Mike McCormick, Greg Minton, Mark Davis, Johnnie LeMaster and Joel Youngblood.

Willie Mays - *Considered by many fans and baseball experts to be the best all-around player in history. Willie possessed all of the rare five tools of baseball and excelled in each of them as he constantly astonished fans and fellow players with his hitting, running and unsurpassed fielding ability.*

(Photo courtesy of National Baseball Hall-of-Fame Library, Cooperstown, N.Y.)

Willie McCovey - *The most feared hitter of his era. "Stretch" consistently delivered key hits in clutch situations. In all, he smashed 521 career home runs, including 18 grand slams. Always a fan favorite, Willie is perhaps the most popular player in San Francisco Giants' history.*

(Photo courtesy of National Baseball Hall-of-Fame Library, Cooperstown, N.Y.)

Juan Marichal - *The greatest pitcher in San Francisco Giants' history. He dominated Major League Baseball in the 1960s by posting an amazing 191 wins, best for the decade. His dominance carried over into All-Star competition as he was untouchable by American League batters in each outing.*

(Photo courtesy of National Baseball Hall-of-Fame Library, Cooperstown, N.Y.)

Gaylord Perry - *The most consistent and reliable pitchers for the Giants' throughout the 1960s and into the 1970s. He was a staff workhorse that threw close to or over 300 innings per season for several years.*

(Photo courtesy of National Baseball Hall-of-Fame Library, Cooperstown, N.Y.)

Orlando Cepeda - *This slugger that appeared in San Francisco the same year the Giants did, 1958. Known as the "Baby Bull" and "Cha-Cha," Cepeda was a solid run producer for the Giants until injuries began to plague him the mid 1960s. Cepeda has always been a real fan favorite.*

(Photo courtesy of National Baseball Hall-of-Fame Library, Cooperstown, N.Y.)

Bobby Bonds - *He emerged in 1968, and was the best prospect in the organization to come along in many seasons. Bobby was one of the first true power-speed players in baseball, combing both to be a dominant all-around player. He nearly missed being the first 40-40 player in 1973, as he sat on 39 home runs the last three weeks of the season.*

(Photo courtesy of National Baseball Hall-of-Fame Library, Cooperstown, N.Y.)

Will Clark - *"The Thrill" excited fans when he burst on the scene as a young, stylish first baseman in 1986. An immediate contributor, Will had a solid glove and could hit for power and average. He was a consistent run producer for several seasons in San Francisco and a cornerstone of the club until his departure after the 1993 campaign.*

(Photo courtesy of National Baseball Hall-of-Fame Library, Cooperstown, N.Y.)

Seals Stadium - *The first home of the Giants when they migrated West in 1958. The small minor league park was once the home of the Pacific Coast League San Francisco Seals. The park was state-of-the-art for its era and was always blessed with the best weather in the City.*

(Photo from National Baseball Hall-of-Fame Library Archive, Cooperstown, N.Y.)

Candlestick Park - *The first of the concrete-era baseball stadiums built. Enigmatic to say the least, the park was not conducive to comfort for players or fans due to the wind. The Giants struggled to make it work to their advantage and management struggled to market it to the public.*

(Photo courtesy of National Baseball Hall-of-Fame Library, Cooperstown, N.Y.)

AT&T Park (Pacific Bell Park / SBC Park) - *Opened in 2000, this facility ranks among the best baseball only venues ever built because of its amenities, style and ambience. The stunning ball yard fits well into the fabric of San Francisco. Its best feature may be the ability for power hitters to smash a ball into McCovey Cove / San Francisco Bay.*

(Photo courtesy of Digital Sky Aerial Imaging.)

Barry Bonds – *Bonds was considered the most extraordinary player of his generation, perhaps of all-time, until he was surrounded by controversy. His dominance, even to and advanced age over 40, was unrivaled. He constantly astonished fans and fellow players with his monstrous home run power and hitting ability.*

(Photo courtesy of Mike Rucki / National Baseball Hall-of-Fame Library, Cooperstown, N.Y.)

Chapter 8: Revitalization and New Success (1990-1997)

Unusual and Rare 1-0 Games: 1973 / 1991

New York Mets' shortstop Kaz Matsui led off a game on May 12, 2004 with a home run off of Randy Johnson and the Arizona Diamondbacks. According to SABR home run guru David Vincent, this was only the 19th instance in Major League history where the lead-off home run accounted for the only run of the game. Of these 19 occurrences, the San Francisco Giants have had two of them. On April 28, 1973 at St. Louis, Bobby Bonds connected off of Reggie Cleveland enroute to the victory. Jim Willoughby threw a shutout, allowing just four hits, to support the winning effort. On August 7, 1991 at Atlanta, Darren Lewis stroked a Charlie Leibrandt pitch over the fence to give his team all the scoring they would need. Bud Black pitched eight solid innings to earn the win. Dave Righetti pitched the ninth inning to earn the save. The pair allowed only six hits to the Atlanta attack.

1993: John Burkett (22) and Billy Swift (21) - Dual 20 Game Winners in 1993

Two right-handed pitchers provided impeccable pitching for the Giants as they drove toward the Western Division title in 1993. Burkett had a 22-win season and Swift a 21-win season. Both pitchers had 34 starts and amassed approximately the same number of innings, 232. Amazingly, this marked the first time that the San Francisco Giants had two 20-game winners in the same season. Unfortunately, the team fell just short of the division championship, losing to Atlanta by one game.

1993: San Francisco Franchise Record 103 Wins (Tie)

The 1993 season was truly magical. New ownership rescued the team, Dusty Baker came on board as manager and Clark, Williams, and Bonds were back-to-back-to-back (3-4-5) in the Giants' lineup. The Giants won a franchise record 103 games while many players had "career" years. However, the Atlanta Braves played at a torrid pace during the last 60 games of the year and edged the Giants out by one game for the division title on the last day of the season. The 1962 National League Champion Giants also won 103 contests (including playoffs).

Will Clark, Career

Will "The Thrill" Clark came into Spring Training in 1986 with only 65 professional games under his belt. His enthusiasm was key in helping the Giants out of the basement of the National League West. Clark demonstrated hitting skill for power and average. He hit a career high 35 home runs in 1987. In 1988, he led the National League in runs batted in with 109. Clark had one of the most potent National League Championship Series ever in 1989 when he batted .650 over a five-game span. He represented the Giants five times in the All-Star Game. Clark ranks in the Top-10 in virtually every San Francisco offensive category. He was selected as a member of the All-1980s and All-1990s San Francisco Giant Team in 1999. Will spent eight seasons in a Giants' uniform. Clark has done some public relations work for the Giants since his retirement after the 2000 season.

Darren Lewis: Errorless Game / Chance Streak from Start of Career and History

Darren Lewis had one for the best starts from a defensive perspective of any player in baseball history. In 1993, Lewis set a Major League record for consecutive games by an outfielder without a miscue, at 267 games. Lewis also set a record for errorless chances by an outfielder with 631. In 1995, he extended his own Major League record for consecutive errorless games (392) and chances (938) before booting a ball and committing the first error of his career on a groundball single versus Montreal on June 30.

Mike Benjamin: Major League Record for Most Base Hits in Three Consecutive Games (1995)

Reserve infielder Mike Benjamin had a extraordinary streak at the plate in June 1995. In the span of three games (June 11-14) he broke the Major League record for most base hits in three consecutive games with 14. He also tied the Major League record for most base hits in two consecutive games with 10 on June 13-14. During the streak, Benjamin tied the all-time San Francisco single-game franchise record for hits in a game with six (13 innings) on June 14 at Chicago. Not known for his hitting, Benjamin had a .196 batting average as a Giant and an overall career average of .229.

Deion Sanders, Career

Although he only played part of one season (1995), and 52 games as a Giant, it would be a glaring omission to not mention possibly the greatest all-around athlete of the generation and last century. He was simply know as "Prime Time" or "Neon Deion" and needed no introduction. His greatest gift was blazing speed that was deadly for opponents on any field. He gained his sports fame as a football player and was regarded by many as the best cover cornerback and kick returner ever to play professional football. There was nothing he could not do on the football field. As a baseball player, Sanders was not nearly as accomplished. By his own admission, he was still learning the game several years into his career. His resume includes: two-time All-American at Florida State in football (1987-88); played in the College World Series; seven-time NFL All-Pro cornerback with Atlanta, San Francisco, Dallas and Baltimore; led the Major Leagues in triples (14) with Atlanta in 1992 and hit .533 in the World Series the same year; played on two Super Bowl champions (San Francisco XXIX, and Dallas XXX). He is the only player in Super Bowl history to have both a pass reception and interception. Sanders also became the first two-way starter in NFL since Chuck Bednarik in 1962. He is the only athlete to play in both World Series and Super Bowl. Hit .285 with five home runs for the Giants.

The Quest for a New Ballpark, Part Two - Proposition B

In March 1996, a fifth measure relating to a new baseball stadium for San Francisco was on the ballot; the previous four had failed. The difference this time was that this was going to be a privately financed stadium, the first in America since Dodger Stadium opened in 1962. The measure easily passed with an acceptance level of 67 percent. The wheels were now in motion to build a new home park for the Giants.

Broadcaster: Hank Greenwald

Hank Greenwald is a broadcaster that fans will never forget. Greenwald had his own distinctive style when it came to baseball play-by-play. He invoked sarcasm and dry humor within his broadcast style with effectiveness. At the time of his retirement from the Giants in 1996, Greenwald had worked 2,798 consecutive Major League games. He went on to chronicle his experiences with a book entitled "This ©opyrighted Broadcast." Greenwald came out of retirement in 2004 to call Oakland A's games for television.

Matt Williams, Career

Matt Williams provided the Giants with solid defensive play and a powerful bat during his tenure at third base. Although he started slow offensively, by the time the '90s came around, Williams was recognized and respected as one of the premier power hitters in the game. In the strike shortened season of 1994, Williams had clubbed 43 home runs in 112 games; he was on pace to break Roger Maris' all-time home run mark for a season, at that time (61) prior to the other sluggers that challenged and eventually broke the mark. Williams is in the Top-10 of most career offensive categories for San Francisco. He was a popular fan favorite. He was selected as a member of the All-1980s, All-1990s and All-Time San Francisco Giant Team in 1999. Matty played 10 seasons for San Francisco.

Robby Thompson, Career

Robby Thompson was one of the steadiest players to ever wear a Giants' uniform. A variety of injuries, including chronic back pain, plagued Thompson for a good part of his career. However, Thompson would play through the pain at his customary second base position and never complain. Thompson is in the Top-10 of most career offensive categories for San Francisco. He was selected as a member of the All-1980s and All-

Time San Francisco Giant Team in 1999. After spending his entire 11 year career with the Giants, Thompson went on to a successful coaching career in Major League baseball.

Lou Seal: Admired Giant's Mascot

After the disaster of Crazy Crab, it took the Giants a few seasons to embark upon the reintroduction of a mascot into their organization. After a lot of razzmatazz and nickname suggestions, the new Giants' mascot made its debut at a game versus the New York Mets on Saturday, April 5, 1997. "Lou Seal," the name chosen out of 1,500 entries, was born. Few people know that his full name is actually Luigi Francisco, a "si-seal-ian" name amazingly submitted by nine separate fans from the Bay Area. Some other interesting names that fans offered included Shaquille O'Seal, Lefty, Say Hey, Cisco, Barky and Mel Otter. "It's a good, tough San Francisco name," said Giants Vice President Pat Gallagher. "The type of name you might find at Fisherman's Wharf or on one of the waterfront piers." The seal, chosen among four finalists in a tryout at Pier 39 in March, 1997, was born and raised in North Beach. Its favorite songs include "Louie, Louie," "Lucille," and "Sealed with a Kiss." His favorite food is crab Louie (what else?). Veteran *San Francisco Examiner* sports editor Glenn Schwarz threw out the first ball that day, with Lou Seal waiting behind the plate. At first some thought that Lou looked more like a rat or rodent. Always animated, he has been popular with fans, and especially children, from the beginning.

09/18/97: Brian Johnson Dramatic Home Run vs. Los Angeles

Late into the 1997 season, the Giants were battling, who else, the Los Angels Dodgers for a playoff spot. They had battled the Dodgers for the whole summer and then hit a slump. By the time Los Angeles visited Candlestick Park in mid-September for a three- game series, the Giants were three games behind. The Giants took the first two games of the series. At the Thursday afternoon finale, the teams were tied entering the bottom of the twelfth inning in a classic confrontation. With fans on the edge of their seats, catcher Brian Johnson blasted a home run in the bottom of the frame to give the Giants a 6-5 win over the Dodgers and a tie for the lead in the National League West. Johnson jumped on the first pitch he saw from reliever Mark Guthrie and planted it in the left field bleachers. The victory catapulted the Giants into a first-place tie and sent 52,140 fans into delirium. Relief pitcher Rod Beck seemingly gave the game away earlier by surrendering three singles (Piazza, Karros and Mondesi) in the 10th inning. Amid a shower of boos, he knuckled-down to strikeout Todd Zeile and induced Eddie Murray into grounding into a 4-2-3 double play. This was voted the favorite 1990s Memory by fans in a website ballot vote in 2003.

1997: Inter-League Play Begins, Giants Success Over the Years

The long debate about inter-league play between the American and National Leagues was finally addressed. In 1997, teams from the National and American Leagues met in regular season play in games that counted in the standings for the first time ever. The Giants' game versus the Texas Rangers, played June 12, 1997 at the Ballpark in Arlington (first pitch 7:11 p.m. CDT), marked the first inter-league contest in Major League history. Teams from like divisions played each other (i.e., NL West vs. AL West, etc.) The original plan called for the divisions to rotate each year. Not until the 2002 season did the divisional play rotation commence and become the norm. The Giants have enjoyed success when playing their American League rivals, sporting a better than .550 win percentage, good for the top-five in Major League Baseball.

1997: Kent, Snow and Bonds, Only 100 RBI Trio in San Francisco History

The Giants have had some of the game's biggest thumpers play for them over the years. Those stars have hit home runs in bushels and driven in runs in droves. However, on only one occasion has there been a group of three players who each achieved the 100 runs batted in plateau in the same season. In 1997, Jeff Kent (121), J.T. Snow (104) and Barry Bonds (101) each bested the century mark, giving the club one of the most potent offenses in the Big Leagues.

1997: National League Western Division Champions

The Giants put it all together and won the National League Western Division title for just the fourth time in their history in 1997. The team was led by Barry Bonds with a .291 batting average, 40 home runs and 101. Young Shawn Estes was a pleasant pitching surprise as he notched 19 wins, over 200 innings pitched, and 181 strikeouts; Rod Beck had 37 saves.

1997 National League Divisional Playoff Series vs. Florida

The Giants faced the Florida Marlins, National League Wild Card Champion, in the Divisional Playoff series. The Marlins were an expansion team in just their fifth year of existence. Giant killer Kevin Brown shut down San Francisco in Game 1, 2-1. Game 2 was also another one-run defeat, with Florida winning for the second consecutive day in the bottom of the ninth inning. The Marlins came to San Francisco and wrapped-up the series with a 6-2 win in Game 3, despite Jeff Kent's three hits.

Rod Beck, Career

One of the most overpowering closers during his era was Rod Beck. He rewrote the Giant record books for saves in a season when he collected an amazing 48 saves in 1993. During that 1993 season Beck only had four blown saves and set, what were then a National League record 24 consecutive and a Major League record 41 consecutive games, stretching into the 1995 campaign. He was selected as a member of the All-1990s and All-Time San Francisco Giant Team in 1999. Beck has the second most saves in club history with 199. Beck played seven seasons in San Francisco.

Chapter 9: The Era of a New Game and Goodbye (1998-1999)

1999: Fearsome Fivesome with the Lumber - Burks, Kent, Bonds, Snow and Aurilia (Equal 1963 Squad)

The 1999 edition of the San Francisco Giants scored a remarkable eight hundred and seventy two runs. This was the second most for the franchise since 1930. The club had plenty of sluggers who could swing the lumber. Barry Bonds (34), Ellis Burks (31), J.T. Snow (24), Jeff Kent (23) and Rich Aurilia (22) became only the second 20 home run quintet in San Francisco history when they tallied 134 between them. The other group, in 1963, boasted three future Hall-of-Famers and two everyday players with pop in their bats. McCovey (44), Mays (38), Cepeda (34), Bailey (21) and F. Alou (20) clubbed a remarkable 157 home runs between them. The 1999 group became the first fivesome to each collect at least 80 runs batted in.

1999: Only 80 Runs Batted in Quartet (Actually a Quintet) in Franchise History

Prior to 1999, only one other Giants' quartet had amassed 80 runs batted in or more in the same season. In 1970, McCovey (126), Dietz

(107), Henderson (88) and Mays (83) achieved it. On the power of their twenty-plus home runs, the 1999 fivesome achieved it, with Aurilia ending up at the 80 RBI mark. The totals were: Kent (101), Snow (98), Burks (96), Bonds (83) and Aurilia (80).

Barry Bonds: *Sporting News* 1990s Baseball Player of the Decade

Like his Godfather Willie Mays before him, Barry Bonds earned the prestigious honor of being named *The Sporting News* 1990s Baseball Player of the Decade. During the 10 year span, Bonds had a .302 batting average (1,478 / 4,894), 1,091 runs scored, 299 doubles, 42 triples, 361 home runs, 1,076 runs batted in, and 343 stolen bases in 1,434 games. Bonds had the third highest RBI total for the period, earned a phenomenal eight Gold Gloves on defense, three Most Valuable Player awards and was selected for the National League All-Star team nine times.

Candlestick Park: Final Game and Closure

On Thursday, September 30, 1999, the Giants played their final game at Candlestick Park against the Los Angeles Dodgers. This culminated 40 years of games at the storied stadium located on the edge of town. The Dodgers spoiled the party by winning 9-4 before a regular season record crowd of 61,389. The Giants held a memorable closing ceremony with numerous Giant alumni present to join in on the celebration festivities. Some interesting final statistics and facts about the stadium:

Selected "Lasts"

National Anthem:	Donna Jean Godcheaux McKay, Phil Lesh, and Bob Weir (part of the original Grateful Dead recording group)
Ceremonial First Pitch:	Juan Marichal
Home Plate Umpire:	Ed Montague
Giant Starter:	Shawn Estes (1st pitch at 1:17 p.m.)
Giant Run Batted In:	Jeff Kent (Bases loaded walk, 5th inning)
Giant Run:	Jay Canizaro (5th inning)
Game Pitch / Swing:	Jeff Shaw (LA) to Marvin Benard (Ground out to 1st base, unassisted)
Home Run:	Raul Mondesi (3-run to left field, 6th inning)
Giant Home Run:	Marvin Benard (Solo to left field, 1st inning)
Run Batted In:	Adrian Beltre (Single to left field, 8th inning)
Hit / Giant Hit:	Ramon Martinez (Single, 9th inning)
"Final" Pitch:	Willie Mays (Low and outside) to Barry Bonds (Catcher / godson)

Overall Totals (Including Post Season)

Games Played:	3,189
Giants' Wins:	1,784
Giants' Losses:	1,405
Giants' Winning %:	.559
Total Home Runs:	5,315
Giants' Home Runs:	2,789
Opponent's Home Runs:	2,526
Attendance:	54,833,242

Season Average (40 years):   1,350,781

Game Average (40 years):   18,097 (3,030 dates)

Other Interesting Approximates

♦ Total Distance of Home Runs: 1,834,920 feet or 362.4 miles (5,315 HR x 360 foot average)

♦ Total Game Time: 8,504 hours or nearly 355 complete days (3,189 games x 2 hours, 40 minutes average game length)

♦ Errors Committed: Approximately 2,775 (3,189 games x 0.87 errors per average game)

♦ Pitches Thrown: Approximately 908.865 (3,189 games x 285 per average game)

♦ Baseballs Used: Approximately 229,608 (3,189 games x six dozen per average game)

Source: *San Francisco Chronicle*, 1999

Historical Baseball Occurrence Note

Bob Watson of the Houston Astros scored Major League Baseball's one-millionth all-time run on May 4, 1975. Watson scored the run on Milt May's three-run home run in the top of the second inning, as part of the Astro's 8-6 loss in the first game of a doubleheader. John Montefusco was the pitcher.

Last Day at Candlestick Park: Closing Ceremony - "Going Away Party" and "Tell It Goodbye"

After the conclusion of the very last baseball game ever played at Candlestick Park, the Giants hosted a final goodbye ceremony to celebrate the 40 years of memorable moments and the players associated with them. The ceremony was hosted by then longtime Giants' Hall-of-Fame radio broadcaster Lon Simmons and the current voice of the Giants Jon Miller of KNBR 680 AM. Simmons' association with the team goes back to the inaugural year of 1958 with the legendary

Russ Hodges on the former flagship station KSFO 560 AM. The pair introduced many former Giants' players, managers and personnel. The group then took one last lap around the stadium to bid farewell.

<u>Giants Alumni at Final Ceremony</u>
(In Order of Introduction)

Mike Sadek
Fred Breining
Carl Boles
Tito Fuentes
Chris Speier
Alan Gallagher
Ken Henderson
Greg Minton
Hobie Landrith
Joey Amalfitano
Don Rose
Terry Whitfield
Billy North
Mike LaCoss
Don Carrithers
Mark Leonard
Jeffrey Leonard
Mike Aldrete
Rich Murray
Butch Metzger
Charlie Fox (Manager)
Herman Franks (Manager)
Dave Kingman
Don Landrum
Jim Barr
Matty Alou
Jesus Alou
Rob Andrews

Mike Ivie
Johnnie LeMaster
Bill Laskey
Atlee Hammaker
Bill Madlock
Bob Knepper
Brett Butler
Garry Maddox
Gary Lavelle
Bill Rigney (Manager)
Mike Murphy (Clubhouse)
Hank Sauer
Ed Halicki
Scott Garrelts
Stu Miller
Dave Righetti
Duane Kuiper
Mike Krukow
Robby Thompson
Dave Dravecky
Roger Craig (Manager)
Vida Blue
Jack Hiatt
Darrell Evans
Jack Clark
Mike McCormick
Bobby Bonds
Orlando Cepeda
Jim Davenport (Attended game then left early- injured)
Juan Marichal
Willie McCovey (Attended game then left early- injured)
Willie Mays

Special "Final" Notes about Candlestick Park

♦ The famed Beatles performed their final public concert on Monday, August 29, 1966 at Candlestick Park as a non-sellout crowd braved the frigid summer night.

♦ Pope John Paul II celebrated Roman Catholic Mass on September 18, 1987 during his United States tour. Giants' shortstop Chris Speier was one of a select few to receive Holy Communion from the Holy Pontiff.

♦ The ball that Willie Mays used to toss the "final" pitch was then set aside to be used for the ceremonial first pitch at Pacific Bell Park on Opening Day of the 2000 season. During the winter / off-season the ball was dubbed "Stitches" and displayed in a traveling showcase to fans all over Northern California.

♦ After the conclusion of the celebration festivities, the Giants' groundskeepers dug-up home plate. It was then placed in the protective custody of the California Highway Patrol. Using one of their helicopters, they immediately shuttled the plate directly to the site of the new ballpark, 3rd and King Streets, for placement in its new "home." Fans watched the whole scene, as it was all caught on camera and shown on the video board at Candlestick Park. The plate was used for just the first game at Pacific Bell Park and then retried.

Candlestick Park: Movie Star (Sort of)

"Experiment in Terror" (1962)

Starring Glenn Ford and Lee Remick

The plot starts with Kelly Sherwood, who is terrorized by a man with an asthmatic voice who plans to use her to steal $100,000 from the bank where she works. He threatens to kill her teenage sister Toby, if she tells the police. However, Kelly manages to contact FBI agent John Ripley for assistance. The climax of this black and white thriller culminates during a crowded night baseball game at Candlestick Park. The criminal is chased through throngs of baseball fans and eventually captured on the pitcher's mound.

"The Enforcer" (1976)

Starring Clint Eastwood and Tyne Daley

In this third installment of the "Dirty Harry" series, Detective Callahan wages war on a terrorist group and his by-the-books superiors. His partner for this mission is a determined female officer who refuses to be bullied by male-chauvinist cops. Callahan and his partner save the mayor, Dirty Harry style. Just prior to being kidnapped, the Mayor of San Francisco can be seen watching part of a Giants' game at Candlestick Park and then leave via his limousine.

"The Fan" (1996)

Starring Robert De Niro and Wesley Snipes

Three-time MVP baseball player Bobby Rayburn joins San Francisco Giants. Gil Renard, an obsessive fan, whose profession is selling hunting knives, is excited over that. But Rayburn is having the worst season of his career and Renard tries to do everything to help him, but goes way too far. This movie, with a horrible plot, stars one of the best actors of his generation and for all-time, in De Niro. Candlestick Park is featured prominently in many game action scenes where Rayburn can be seen batting and playing left field. The similarities between Rayburn and Barry Bonds are sometimes eerie.

"The Rock" (1996)

Starring Sean Connery and Nicholas Cage

A group of renegade United States Marine commandos seizes a stockpile of lethal chemical weapons and takes over Alcatraz Island in San Francisco Bay, with 81 tourists as hostages. Their leader, a former highly-decorated General, demands a $100 million ransom, as restitution to families of soldiers who died in covert operations and were thereby denied compensation. If the authorities fail to pay, he threatens to launch 15 rockets carrying the deadly VX nerve gas into the Bay Area. An elite Navy SEAL team, with support from an FBI chemical warfare expert and a former Alcatraz prisoner / escapee, is assembled to penetrate the terrorists' defenses on Alcatraz and neutralize the rockets threat before time runs out. A sold-out 49ers game at Candlestick Park is the first target of the renegades.

Popular Giants' Broadcast Team: Kruk (Mike Krukow) and Kuip (Duane Kuiper)

Duane Kuiper and Mike Krukow were popular players when they played for the Giants. After they established themselves in their new career as broadcasters, they are even more popular. Kuiper went on to become an excellent play-by-play announcer for the club. Krukow provided expert commentary and mirth as a color commentator. The two made a wonderful duo that provided much listening enjoyment for Giants' fans everywhere.

Major League Baseball All 20th Century Honor Teams / Lists

As the 20th Century closed, many baseball experts, organizations and Major League Baseball itself sought to honor the players that stared in the game during the past 100-year stretch. As expected, many San Francisco Giants' players adorned these lists. Below are the selected members. Some players listed played a majority of their careers for other teams, but played at least one season with San Francisco in their career.

Major League Baseball All-Century Team Nominees

Pitcher

Steve Carlton	(8th - 405,365 votes)
Warren Spahn	(10th - 337,215 votes)
Juan Marichal	(20th - 122,366 votes)

1st Base

Willie McCovey	(7th - 106,717 votes)

2nd Base

Joe Morgan	(2nd - 608,660 votes)

Outfield

Willie Mays	(4th - 1,115,896 votes)
Barry Bonds	(18th - 173,279 votes)
Duke Snider	(24th - 63,410 votes)

100 Greatest Baseball Players of the 20th Century

Source: *The New Bill James Historical Abstract*

3. Willie Mays
15. Joe Morgan
16. Barry Bonds
36. Warren Spahn
50. Duke Snider
69. Willie McCovey
78. Steve Carlton

100 Greatest Baseball Players of the 20th Century

Source: *The Sporting News*

2. Willie Mays
21. Warren Spahn
30. Steve Carlton
34. Barry Bonds
56. Willie McCovey
60. Joe Morgan
71. Juan Marichal
83. Duke Snider
97. Gaylord Perry

100 Greatest Baseball Players of the 20th Century

Source: *Society For American Baseball Research (SABR)*

8. Willie Mays
15. Warren Spahn
30. Steve Carlton
37. Joe Morgan
58. Juan Marichal
62. Willie McCovey
65. Barry Bonds
68. Duke Snider

Top 10 Baseball Players of the 20th Century, by Position

Source: *The New Bill James Historical Abstract*

Catcher
8. Gary Carter

1st Base
9. Willie McCovey

2nd Base
1. Joe Morgan

3rd Base
10. Darrell Evans

Left Field
3. Barry Bonds

Center Field
1. Willie Mays

Left Hand Pitcher
2. Warren Spahn
5. Steve Carlton

Bullpen Closer
3. Rich "Goose" Gossage
5. Dan Quisenberry

Chapter 10: Embarking on a New Century (2000-2006)

Pacific Bell Park: Part One - Part of the City Fabric and Skyline

Like many of the new "older" or retro baseball parks it designed throughout the country, HOK Sports of Kansas City created a unique sports venue for the city of San Francisco. The glistening park, which opened in 2000, features panoramic views of downtown San Francisco, the San Francisco / Oakland Bay Bridge, and San Francisco Bay itself. The original capacity was a cozy 40,930. Renamed SBC Park in 2004 and AT&T Park in 2006

Pacific Bell Park: Part Two - Character and Nuances

The design of Pacific Bell Park contains many unique characteristics and nuances that are not present at any other baseball park in the world. The right field wall is only 309 feet from home plate. A good poke over that wall and the promenade by a hard-hitting slugger and the ball lands in the Bay (McCovey Cove). There is a three-story Coca-Cola bottle with children's slides inside of it in left field; this is next to the huge old-time, four finger baseball glove. Fans who do not have tickets for the game can watch through chain link fence cutouts in right field.

Pacific Bell Park: Part 3 - Joins The Big Leagues in a Unique Way

Amid the pomp and circumstance of Opening Day at Pacific Bell Park, a unique ritual occurred that officially ensued that the infield had joined the Major Leagues. Parachute jumpers landed in the ballpark with dirt samplings in their possession from **all** of the 29 other Major League baseball stadiums. Wes Krukow, son of Giants' broadcaster and former 20-game winner Mike Krukow, spearheaded the collection effort. He joined members of the Junior Giants and the groundskeepers in scattering the soil on the new field. Father Floyd Lotito from San Francisco's Saint Boniface Catholic Church then blessed Pacific Bell Park and this unique mixture of dirt.

The Name Game

The home filed of the Giants in downtown San Francisco has had a few names during its young life. This was due to corporate mergers and takeovers. From its construction stage until the end of the 2003 season, the park was known as Pacific Bell Park. For the 2004 and 2005 campaigns, the park was named SBC Park. From 2006 on, the park has been named AT&T Park. For the purpose of clarity and logic this book, the park will be referred to the name it possessed during that specific season, unless noted.

04/11/00: Opening Game at Pacific Bell Park vs. Los Angeles

After much fanfare, the Giants opened their new jewel at 3rd and King streets against the rival Los Angeles Dodgers. A sellout crowd of 40,930 was on hand to celebrate. However, shortstop Kevin Elster spoiled the show by smacking three home runs and led the Dodgers to a 6-5 victory. His three home runs were the first in the inaugural game at a park by a player in Major League history. In all, the Giants lost their first six games in the new yard before achieving victory. The first win came on April 29 against the Montreal Expos, 2-1. Barry Bonds belted the game-winning home run in the bottom of the eighth inning. This was the first "official" game played at the park that counted in the standings. The Giants had played two exhibition games in the previous week against the Milwaukee Brewers and the New York Yankees.

Selected "Firsts"

All Pacific Bell and Giants' firsts occurred during the home opener on April 11, 2000 versus the Los Angeles Dodgers (unless otherwise noted with date in description).

National Anthem:
Bobby McFerrin

Ceremonial First Pitch:
Peter Magowan and Larry Baer

First Pitch (time):
1:39 p.m.

First Pitch (outcome):
Ball (Thrown by Kirk Rueter to Devon White)

Home Plate Umpire:
Ed Montague

Time of Game:
3:01

First Night Game:
Wednesday, April 12, 2000 (vs. Los Angeles)

Giants' Hitting Firsts

Batter (outcome):
Marvin Benard (Flyout to right field)

Hit:
Bill Mueller (Single through hole at 2nd base, 1st inning)

Run Scored:
Bill Mueller, (Scored from 1st base on Barry Bonds' double, 1st inning)

Home Run:
Barry Bonds (Solo shot to center field in 3rd inning, 2-2 pitch)

Run Batted In:
Barry Bonds (Double to right field, scoring Bill Mueller, 1st inning)

Grand Slam:
Bobby Estalella (To left field, 4th inning, 05/02/00)

Pinch-Hit Home Run:
Calvin Murray (To left field, 7th inning, 04/13/00)

Inside the Park Home Run:
Dustin Mohr ("Hit the Car" on left field wall, 5th inning, 08/04/04)

Giants' Pitching Firsts

Strikeout:
Kirk Rueter (Mark Grudzielanek, 1st inning)

Complete Game:
Livan Hernandez, (9.0 innings vs. Arizona, 04/14/00)

Giants' Fielding Firsts

Putout:
Doug Mirabelli (Caught 3rd strike on batter Mark Grudzielanek, 1st inning)

Assist:

Kirk Rueter and J.T. Snow (Assisting Jeff Kent on caught stealing of Devon White, 1st inning)

The First "Splash" Hit at Pacific Bell Park

Monday, May 1, 2000 was a balmy night as the Giants hosted the New York Mets at Pacific Bell Park. In the sixth inning, Barry Bonds thrilled the crowd when he connected on a pitch off of the Mets' Rich Rodriguez (an ex-Giant). The towering blast sailed over the right field wall, and promenade into the water at McCovey Cove for the first, long awaited, official "splash" into the Bay in Pacific Bell Park history. In an exhibition game on April 1, Bonds connected off New York Yankee hurler Andy Pettitte.

2000 Season: Giants Enjoy the Comforts of Pacific Bell Park

The San Francisco Giants moved into their new home, Pacific Bell Park, for the 2000 season. During that inaugural campaign, the Giants enjoyed the best regular season record in all of Major League baseball, posting a 97-65 record, for a winning percentage of .599. This marked the first time since 1962 that the Giants had the best record in all of Major League Baseball. Additionally, the team tied for the best home win/loss record (New York Mets) at 55-26, for an amazing .679 winning percentage (it should be noted that one of the Mets "home" losses came while in Japan to open the season). This is in spite of the fact that the team lost their first six games played at the new field and had an eight-game losing streak on the road in mid-May. The Giants' pitchers also enjoyed the new park, as San Francisco owned the best home earned-run average in all of Major League Baseball with a mark of 3.45 (3.27 *after* their initial six losses).

2000 National League Divisional Playoff Series vs. New York

The team opened the National Divisional Playoff Series with the New York Mets, the Wild Card Champion. The Giants, lead by Livan Hernandez's pitching masterpiece, took the first game of the series 5-1. The San Francisco offense was ignited by Ellis Burks's three-run home run. After this, the Mets shut down the Giant offense with some brilliant and unlikely pitching; the Giants' did not muster a single run in the last 18 innings of the series, which included two extra-inning heartbreaking defeats. New York won the series three games to one.

Jeff Kent: 2000 National League Most Valuable Player

The 2000 season for Jeff Kent was truly a classic career year. Voted the National League's Most Valuable Player, Kent became only the eighth second baseman in Major League history to garner the honor. Kent beat out teammate Barry Bonds, marking the 11th time in National League history (second for the Giants: Mitchell / Clark, 1989) that situation had occurred. Kent's numbers included a .334 batting average, 33 home runs and 125 runs batted in. Jeff ranked among the leaders in nearly every offensive category: RBI (4th), batting average (6th), runs scored (8th), hits (5th), extra base hits (T-6th), batting average with RISP (6th), slugging percentage (10th), on-base percentage (6th) and multi-hit game (T-6th). He posted career highs in eight of those categories.

Broadcaster: Jon Miller

Jon Miller has the lucky job of being a broadcaster for a Major League team. However, it goes beyond that for Miller, as he is also the broadcaster of his favorite childhood team, the San Francisco Giants. Miller grew up in the Bay Area and was a fan of the team; he grew up idolizing two great Giants' broadcasters: Russ Hodges and Lon Simmons. Miller honed his skills by "broadcasting" mock games and bringing his tape recorder to Oakland A's games and practicing from the bleachers. Miller was also recognized as a top broadcaster on a national level, having done the ESPN Sunday Night Game of the Week for many years with his partner, Bay Area native and former Giant, Joe Morgan.

Broadcaster: Lon Simmons

Lon Simmons joined the Giants' family when they arrived from New York in 1958. He immediately joined the Hall-of-Fame broadcaster Russ Hodges and formed a memorable announcing duo that was together until Hodges' death in 1971. Simmons was a fixture and favorite in the Bay Area for decades. In addition to working for the Giants, Simmons also broadcasted for the San Francisco 49ers, Oakland Athletics, and even the Winter Olympics (ice hockey - Squaw Valley, 1960). Simmons is best known for his trademark home run call, "Tell it Goodbye." Lon retired to Maui, Hawaii after the 2002 season. In 2004, Lon was rewarded with the prestigious Ford C. Frick Award for excellence in baseball broadcasting and enshrined in the Broadcast Wing of the Hall-of-Fame.

Dave Righetti: Player and Coach

When Dave Righetti joined the San Francisco Giants in 1991, he came home. Righetti grew up in nearby San Jose, and as a child was a Giants' fan. Righetti enjoyed a great career in which he was originally a starting pitcher and then developed into one of the game's finest closers for years. His 252 career saves ranks 21st on the all-time Major League list. On Independence Day 1983, Righetti threw the first Yankee no-hitter since Don Larsen (1956 World Series). Dave returned to the Giants' organization in 1999 as a roving instructor and joined Dusty Baker's staff in 2000 as pitching coach. He continued in the same role when Felipe Alou came on board. Dave pitched three seasons for the Giants.

Arizona Connection: Spring Training (Casa Grande / Phoenix / Scottsdale)

The Giants began their relationship with the Valley of the Sun when they were still based in New York, back in 1947. The Cactus League became a reality that year, when Horace Stoneham's New York Giants and Bill Veeck's Cleveland Indians took up residence in Phoenix and Tucson, respectively. That Veeck ended up in Tucson was not a surprise. He owned ranches in the Southwest and at the time owned a ranch near Tucson. Stoneham was a natural for Phoenix, as he developed business interests in the area. Every year (with the exception of 1951, when the team trained in St. Petersburg, Florida) since then, the Giants have arrived to start their journey on the road to a National League Pennant. Throughout the 1950s and '60s Casa Grande served as a training spot and the Giants played their home games at Phoenix Municipal Stadium, the home of their Triple-A minor league affiliate Phoenix Giants of the Pacific Coast League. In 1982, the team picked up stakes and moved to the nearby suburb of Phoenix, Scottsdale. They played in old Scottsdale Stadium for many years. Spring Training became a popular vacation destination for fans due to its close proximity to the Bay Area. In 1996, the community built a wonderful new park and facility that could accommodate larger crowds. The Giants still call it home today.

Blockbuster Trades Throughout the Years

For many fans, the most memorable trades that the Giants have made through the years leave them with a feeling of injustice. The trades that sent Orlando Cepeda, Gaylord Perry, and Willie McCovey away were controversial because those players still had productive years remaining in their careers. The players the team received in return were questionable and certainly did not meet expectations. Fans will never forget where they were on the day that the Giants traded Willie Mays back to New York, to the Mets at the end of his career. Perhaps two of the "worst" trades in San Francisco history were deals in which two future stars were shipped out: Steve Stone, a future Cy Young Award winner and George

Foster, a future 50-plus home run hitter. On the other hand, the seven-player trade (plus $390,000) for Vida Blue in 1978 was one of the best in franchise history and immediately paid dividends.

Giants' Community Relations Programs: ("Until There's a Cure", etc.)

Over the 50 years in San Francisco, the Giants have become a part of the community fabric of the City. The Giants have always maintained a good relationship with their fans and the community. The Giants have recognized the diversity that makes up the entire San Francisco / Oakland / San Jose / Bay Area and boasted one of the premier community relations and outreach programs in professional sports. The Giants have had countless "days" at the ballparks recognizing different charity, ethnic, civic, education, and non-profit groups.

The Giants have supported reading programs for students, baseball leagues / fields for underprivileged children and anti-violence programs, to name a few. In 1994, the Giants became the first-ever professional sports team to host an AIDS awareness and benefit game with "Until There's a Cure Day." This has since become an annual tradition. Some of the other popular and ongoing programs include: the Giants' Community Fund, Junior Giants, Strike Out Violence and the Summer Reading Program.

Giant - Dodger Rivalry: One of the Best in the History of Sports

The Giant-Dodger rivalry goes back to the early part of the 20th Century in the New York-Brooklyn days. When both teams relocated to the Pacific Coast in 1958, nothing changed, and the rivalry remained as intense as ever. During the 1960s and into the early '70s, tempers often their reached boiling point, with bench clearing escapades becoming the norm. The apex of the rivalry was on August 22, 1965. After being nicked on the ear by the return throw to the pitcher, Giants' pitcher Juan Marichal attacked Dodgers' catcher John Roseboro with a bat. It was one of the most violent brawls in sports history. The incident proved costly, as Marichal was suspended for nine games in the midst of the race. The Dodgers went 15-1 down the stretch to edge out the Giants. Over the course of the past 20 years, the rivalry has re-emerged at different times, especially when one or both of the teams are vying for playoff spots.

Giants' Successful Scouting and Minor League Development System

Horace Stoneham was a pioneer in the building of a strong minor league organization. In the 1950s, Stoneham was aided by scouts like George Gonovese and Ed Montague, Sr. who looked for great talent, but also players that could blend well into the team's developmental program. The pair discovered such future stars as Willie Mays, Willie McCovey, Juan Marichal and Orlando Cepeda. Into the 1960s, the good fortune continued, with the signing of such prospects as Gaylord Perry, Bobby Bonds and Jim Ray Hart. This is best exemplified by and Associated Press story in July, 1966. Major League Baseball had 20 teams, with each club having 25 active players. That equals a total of 475 players, not including the Giants' active roster. Of those 475 players, 37 were homegrown San Francisco system products. The Giants were also one of the pioneers in scouting and signing impressive talent from Latin America and the Caribbean.

Hitting for the Cycle: Giants Have Their Share of This Rare Achievement

Hitting for the cycle is a rarity in baseball. Many fans and media personnel overlook this fact. In the entire history of the game, there have been less then 250 occurrences in over 125 years of play. It took a dozen years before the Giants would experience their first in San Francisco, as Jim Ray Hart finally achieved the feat. In San Francisco franchise history, there have been eight players who have hit for the cycle, but only two at home, and none at AT&T Park, thus far.

- ◆ Jim Ray Hart at Atlanta, 07/08/70
- ◆ Dave Kingman at Houston, 04/16/72
- ◆ Jeffrey Leonard at Cincinnati, 06/27/85
- ◆ Candy Maldonado at St. Louis, 05/04/87
- ◆ Chris Speier vs. St. Louis, 07/09/88
- ◆ Robby Thompson vs. San Diego, 04/22/91
- ◆ Jeff Kent at Pittsburgh, 05/03/99
- ◆ Randy Winn at Cincinnati, 08/15/05

Jeff Kent, Career

When the Giants traded popular superstar third baseman Matt Williams to Cleveland, it was very unpopular with the fans. Fans wondered how Kent would fill Williams' shoes. However, fans soon came to find that the trade wasn't that bad. Kent provided much pop and teamed with Barry Bonds to form the best one-two punch for the Giants since the early '60s. He became only the third second baseman of the 20th Century to drive in 100 or more runs in three consecutive seasons (1997-99). Amazingly, he continued into the next century. By the time he left San Francisco after the 2002 season, he had achieved the 100-RBI mark in each of his six seasons here. This was bested in San Francisco by only Willie Mays (eight, '59-'66). Kent was a hard-nosed player that played with a definite style. Jeff spent six seasons in a Giants' uniform.

KNBR 680 / KSFO 560: Giants Flagship Radio Stations for 50 Years

During their 50 years in San Francisco, the Giants have had only two flagship stations broadcast their games. First, in 1958, KSFO, the top station of its era, carried their games into the 1980s. The station's popularity waned and the Giants looked for a new station. They struck a deal with another leading station in the city, KNBR, who had 50,000 watts of broadcast power. The Giants' relationship with KNBR was successful, as the team became a partial, albeit minority, owner of the club as part of the Peter Magowan group purchase in 1993. The Giants' games continue to broadcast on KNBR today.

KTVU Channel 2 / Fox Sports Net: Giants Flagship Television Stations

There is no doubt that television has had a profound impact on the game of baseball. The Giants have had a relationship with the same television station since their arrival in San Francisco. KTVU Channel 2 of Oakland was the sole carrier of Giants' games for many, many years. In the mid-1980s, cable television became a factor that sports had never seen. The explosion led to exponential exposure for all sports. A local Bay Area broadcaster, Fox Sports Net (formally Sports Channel), began broadcasting many Giants' games. Over a period of years, as more cable subscribers emerged, they took responsibility for a majority of the games. The Giants have still maintained a relationship with KTVU, still contracting for the broadcast of several games during the season. Now, virtually every game is available for viewing on television, via some outlet.

Miguel "Mike" Murphy, Career (Clubhouse Manager)

The employee with the longest service with the San Francisco Giants is Miguel "Mike" Murphy. "Murph" has been a fixture in the clubhouse since 1958. He started as a batboy for the Giants while at Seals Stadium, their very first season in San Francisco. When Candlestick Park opened in 1960, Murphy became the visitor's clubhouse attendant. In 1980, he was promoted to equipment manager for the Giants when longtime veteran Eddie Logan retired. Murph has been a devoted employee and has a lifetime of memories. In recognition of his lifelong commitment to the organization, the Giants' clubhouse at Pacific Bell Park is named the "Mike Murphy Clubhouse." Over the years, Murphy has forged friendships with many of the game's all-time great players, including many Giants and other National Leaguers. Murph's office is always one of the favorite stops at the park for Giants' alumni.

Handful of Native San Franciscans Play for the Giants

In all the years that the Giants have been in San Francisco, only a handful of actual natives have played on the field for the club. Names like Alan Gallagher, Fred Breining, and Ken Reitz come to mind. Fans will always remember the style of "Dirty" Al Gallagher at the hot corner. He provided solid defense and exciting play for the club for two seasons in 1970-71. Exciting outfield speedster Willie McGee played more games than any native, logging 444 total in his four seasons in the orange and black. There have been several other players who were natives of the greater San Francisco-Oakland Bay Area that have worn the Giant uniform, but the group listed below consists of only (those) players actually born within the City.

Player	Position	Year(s) w/ Giants	Games w/ Giants
Alan Gallagher	3rd Base	1970 - 73	332
John Boccabella	Catcher	1974	29
Ken Reitz	3rd Base	1976	155
Fred Breining	Pitcher	1980 - 83	136
Mike Vail	Outfield	1983	18
Keith Comstock	Pitcher	1987	15
Willie McGee	Outfield	1991 - 94	444
Jalal Leach	Outfield	2001	8
Tyler Walker	Pitcher	2004 - 06	125

Baseball Rarities and Oddities Over the Years with the Giants

Baseball has always been a game of oddities and the unexpected. There is no end to the unbelievable plays that can and have happened in a baseball game. As we review game scoresheets, we run across many of them. Over the years, the Giants have been involved in their share of the rare and obscure. The analysts at retrosheet.org have done an excellent job of finding many of these. Here are several examples:

♦ General Nature

September 1, 1967 - San Francisco at Cincinnati

No fan can forget the game in 1963 in which Juan Marichal dueled Warren Spahn for 16 innings and was finally victorious 1-0. Later in the decade the Giants' other ace, Gaylord Perry, also pitched 16 innings in a game, which is noteworthy too. This was also a 1-0 game but went a little longer, as it stretched to 21 innings in length. The Giants battled the Cincinnati Reds and eventually emerged triumphant. Unfortunately, Perry did not figure in the decision and have the same reward as Marichal. He Gave way to Frank Linzy who pitched the remaining five frames and picked up the win.

July 20, 1968 - Houston at San Francisco

At age 37, the great Willie Mays scored all the way from first base on a *single* by Jim Ray Hart for the game's only run. A true example of Mays' speed, even at an advancing age. Ray Sadecki held down the Astros for the win.

May 20, 1970 - Philadelphia at San Francisco

In one of the oddest coincidences of all-time, the Philadelphia Phillies lost two catchers to broken hands in the same inning. In the bottom of the sixth, a foul tip on a 2-1 pitch struck Tim McCarver and broke a bone in his hand. Backup catcher Mike Ryan replaced McCarver.

After Willie Mays singled and Willie McCovey stroked an RBI double, Ken Henderson singled to right field. McCovey tried to score and was thrown out at the plate. During the play, Willie spiked Ryan, breaking his hand. Little used utility man Jim Hutto then replaced Ryan.

May 14, 1972 - San Francisco at New York (N)

This was the first game for Willie Mays against the Giants after he was traded to the Mets. The game was played in New York at Shea Stadium. San Francisco starting pitcher Sam McDowell had a wild opening to the game with BB, BB, BB, HR, K, K, K in the score book. Three walks, a grand slam home run and three strike outs. This was the line for the first inning. He allowed no more runs and ended-up with no-decision as the Mets won 5-4. Mays led off and played first base for the Mets. He went 1-for-2 in his return debut in the Big Apple.

May 16, 1972 - Cincinnati at San Francisco (Game 1)

With Dave Concepcion on first base and one out, the Giants attempted to walk Pete Rose intentionally. Rose refused to take the free pass from pitcher Ron Bryant and swung at a pitch that was wide of the strike zone, hitting a grounder to Jim Ray Hart at third base. Hart booted the ball for an error, but Rose was thrown out trying to advance to second base. Concepcion scored what turned out to be the winning run.

May 31, 1972 - Los Angeles at San Francisco

In a month where the Giants were part of many obscurities, things continued to happen. In the top of the fourth inning, all-time great Frank Robinson was on first base with one out for the Dodgers. Los Angeles slugger Wes Parker hit a line shot to the Giants' Bobby Bonds in right field who, with his blazing speed, then sprinted toward first base to double-off Robinson unassisted. This is a rare double play for a right fielder to achieve, due to the distance needed to be covered in a short period of time.

May 20, 1978 - San Francisco at Chicago (N)

In the top of the eighth inning after a Jack Clark single, the game was suspended at 6:34 p.m. due to darkness (Wrigley Field had no lights at that time). Since it was get-away day and the last trip into Wrigley for the Giants that year, the game was completed at Candlestick Park, in San Francisco, on July 28. A most unusual, but not unprecedented, way to complete a game.

May 17, 1980 - St. Louis at San Francisco

Here we have a most unusual play with Ken Reitz batting for the Cardinals in the ninth inning: Keith Hernandez doubled and Ted Simmons singled; George Hendrick singled, advancing Hernandez to third base. The Cardinals had the bases loaded. Reitz then grounded to the shortstop for a force play. However the shortstop decided to throw to the second baseman for the out and Hernandez scored from third base. The unusual part of the play is the absence of a run batted in. The Giants' scoresheet says "run scores on defensive indifference - no RBI." The fielder just forgot about the base runner heading toward home plate. The official totals confirm this and the *San Francisco Chronicle* chastised the Giants for their slow, indecisive play.

September 1, 1985 - New York (N) at San Francisco

In this late-season Sunday afternoon contest, the visiting New York Mets edged the Giants 4-3. Keith Hernandez's two-run pinch home run to the upper deck in right field climaxed a three-run ninth inning. Earlier in the game, in the Mets' half of the fifth inning, a baseball rarity occurred that is rarely seen above the Little League level. Pitcher Ed Lynch lined what seemed to be a single to right field. Playing shallow and reacting quickly, Giants' right fielder Joel Youngblood picked up the ball and fired it to Dan Driessen at first base, and recorded the rare 9-3 putout in the baseball score book. Although rare, it was the National League's second 9-3 putout in two months.

June 7, 1992 - Houston at San Francisco

Pitcher Trevor Wilson attained a baseball rarity when he struck out the side on just the minimum of nine pitches. He achieved this versus the Houston Astros in the ninth inning at Candlestick Park, preserving a 3-0, two-hit shutout. Jeff Bagwell, Eric Anthony and Rafael Ramirez were the victims.

July 22, 1999 - San Diego at San Francisco

Pitcher Jerry Spradlin also completed a rare feat by striking out four batters in one inning. This was a result of a mishandled pitch by catcher Scott Servais. He achieved this against San Diego in the seventh inning at Candlestick Park.

May 2, 2005 - San Francisco at Arizona

ESPN senior writer Jayson Stark uncovered an obscure and outright rare situation in an early season game. Only in baseball can something that is seemingly mathematically impossible actually happen. Relief pitcher Scott Eyre had the following line in a May 2nd game at Arizona:

IP	H	R	ER	BB	K
0	0	1	0	0	1

If you did not know the truth, you would have sworn that this guy did not allow a base runner in the game, but still surrendered a run. Also notice that he had a strikeout, but never did record an actual out. This all started when Mike Matheny neglected to catch a third strike on Shawn Green that would have ended the inning. Green made it to first base on the passed ball. After Eyre departed, Green scored on a double by Tony Clark.

July 28, 2005 - San Francisco at Milwaukee

Brad Hennessey twirled seven shutout innings in a 3-0 blanking of the Milwaukee Brewers at Miller Park. But that was not the only big news of the day. Coupled with his masterful pitching performance was the fact that he also drove in all three runs himself. Hennessey connected for a big fly in the fifth inning with two runners on and two out. How rare is it to have a pitcher hit a three-run home run and account for all three runs in a 3-0 shutout? According to the Elias Sports Bureau, only one other player had ever done it. And that was over a century prior. Pitcher Al Orth of the Philadelphia Phillies achieved this on May 31, 1900. Orth was not a bad player, he had over 200 career wins (at least 100 in each league) and batted .273 for his career. Hopefully Brad can follow in his steps.

August 16, 2005 - San Francisco at Cincinnati

When a player goes 5-5 in a game that is considered a pretty good day. It is not that uncommon, but still a noticeable feat. Now, to have two players from the same team, in the same game achieve this mark, that is indeed extraordinary and unique. In a late-summer game at Cincinnati, both Pedro Feliz and Deivi Cruz had the distinctive line score that jumped off the page. Feliz had two doubles, a triple and scored four runs. Interestingly, he did not have any runs batted-in. Cruz had one double, one home run, scored two runs and had five runs batted-in. The Giants won the game 10-8 in a game they exploded for a 19-hit attack.

♦ Hidden Ball Tricks

It is baseball's most famous act of deception and trickery, and if it is done correctly, results in the victim being greatly embarrassed in addition to making an out. The play was more common in the early days of the game before rules were adopted that limited what the pitcher could do to make it appear that he had the ball when he did not. However, it is far from extinct as can be seen in the list below. Review of historical box scores shows that it has been successfully documented 190 times in baseball history. The Giants have successfully completed the trick five times. They have also been victim on three occasions. Even the great Willie Mays was fooled once.

Hidden Ball Tricks Turned by the Giants					
Date	Inning	Perpetrator(s)	Position(s)	Victim	Team
06/05/58	9th	Orlando Cepeda	1st Base	Wes Covington	Milwaukee
09/04/66	8th	Jim Ray Hart to Hal Lanier	3rd Base 2nd Base	Orlando Cepeda	St. Louis
06/29/80	8th	Rich Murray to Johnny LeMaster	1st Base Shortstop	Dusty Baker	Los Angeles
06/28/94	6th	Matt Williams	3rd Base	Rafael Bournigal	Los Angeles
06/26/99	4th	J. T. Snow	1st Base	Carlos Perez	Los Angeles

Hidden Ball Tricks Turned Against the Giants					
Date	Inning	Perpetrator(s)	Position(s)	Team	Victim
04/26/70	2nd	Bobby Wine	Shortstop	Montreal	Willie Mays
05/18/90	2nd	Delino DeShields	2nd Base	Montreal	Terry Kennedy
06/28/95	1st	Vinny Castilla	3rd Base	Colorado	Darren Lewis

♦ Batting Out of Turn

Occasionally, a player will bat out of turn according to the lineup provided to the umpires by the manager before the game. This can cause great confusion on the part of managers and umpires trying to decide what to do about the mistake. Rule 6.07 discusses, at great length, the concept of batting out of turn. Rule 10.03 (d) discusses the scoring of such plays. If the team at bat does not gain by the illegal action, the opposing manager usually says nothing. However, when that illegal batter does advance the cause of his team by advancing or scoring a runner, then it is time to speak out. This is not always done, however, since many times the opponents are unaware of the mistake. There are 27 instances of this event from 1950 to the present. The Giants have committed the mistake twice.

May 15, 1974 - San Francisco at Cincinnati

The Giants skipped a batter in the eighth inning. In the sixth inning, Bobby Bonds pinch-hit for the pitcher. He stayed in the game in the ninth spot in the order and the new pitcher batted in the first spot. The next time around the order, Bonds hit a home run and Tito Fuentes hit for the pitcher. Mike Phillips should have batted next, but Garry Maddox, the number three hitter, came to the plate instead and made an out. The Reds said nothing in this case and eventually won the game, 4-3.

August 8, 1998 - Atlanta at San Francisco

In the bottom of the fifth inning, the Giants' Shawon Dunston pinch-hit for Ellis Burks in the second spot in the order and ended the inning with a strikeout. In the top of the sixth inning, manager Dusty Baker made five substitutions in his lineup, including leaving Dunston in the game. New players went into the third through fifth spots in the order. Stan Javier started the bottom of the sixth properly and was out. Then Joe Carter and Rich Aurilia got confused and Aurilia batted out of turn. He walked, Carter flew out and then Bill Mueller, who had been in the game, walked. By now it was too late for the Braves (ahead 10-2) to say anything, if they actually knew there was a problem. With all the changes, they might not have realized that Aurilia had batted out of turn. The Giants scored three runs in the inning but lost the game 14-6. Carter and Aurilia hit in the proper order the next time around the lineup in the seventh inning.

♦ Passing Runners on the Bases

According to Official Baseball Rule 7.08 (h), any runner is out if he passes a preceding runner before that runner is out. This is not an appeal play but is called immediately by the umpire. There have been many cases of a runner passing a preceding runner through the years. There have been 49 documented accounts since 1921, with the Giants being guilty twice.

June 19, 1974 - San Francisco at St. Louis

Giant first baseman Ed Goodson hit a home run in the third inning off Bob Gibson at St. Louis with Garry Maddox on first base and no one out. Unfortunately, Goodson passed Maddox between first and second. Goodson was credited with a single and a run batted in. The Giant's still prevailed, 5-4.

May 15, 1985 - Pittsburgh at San Francisco

In San Francisco's side of the second inning, first baseman David Green doubled. Jose Uribe then hit a ground ball to Pirates' shortstop Bill Almon, and Green was caught between second and third base. He eluded the tag, returning to second base, but was passed by Uribe and called out. The visiting Pirates won the contest, 3-2.

♦ Triple Plays Turned by the Giants
* = Actual putout

05/03/65 San Francisco Giants @ St. Louis

Bottom of the 6th - Score 0-3 (two men on: Phil Gagliano 1B, Bill White 2B)
Putout Sequence: 1-6*-3*-2*

Tim McCarver (StL) is the batter. He hits a ground ball to pitcher Ron Herbel who pivots and throws to shortstop Jose Pagan who forces the runner from first base, Phil Gagliano (Out 1), Pagan throws over to Willie McCovey who retires the batter at first base, Tim McCarver (Out 2), McCovey throws home to catcher Tom Haller who, tags out the runner trying to score from second, Bill White (Out 3).

05/02/67 San Francisco Giants @ New York (N)

Bottom of the 2nd - Score 0-0 (two men on: Ed Kranepool 1B, Tommy Davis 2B)
Putout Sequence: 1*-6*-3*

Ken Boyer (NY) is the batter. He hits a hard line drive back to the pitcher Gaylord Perry (Out 1), Perry pivots and throws to the shortstop Hal Lanier who doubles up the runner caught off second base, Tommy Davis (Out 2), Lanier throws over to Willie McCovey, who nabs the runner caught off first, Ed Kranepool (Out 3).

06/21/76 San Francisco Giants @ San Diego

Bottom of the 3rd - Score 0-2 (two men on: Willie Davis 1B, Tito Fuentes 2B)
Putout Sequence: 3*-6*-3*

Willie McCovey (SD) is the batter. He hits a line drive directly to first baseman Darrell Evans (Out 1), Evans throws to shortstop Chris Speier who tags the runner caught off second, Tito Fuentes (Out 2), Speier throws back to Evans, who tags the runner caught off first base, Willie Davis (Out 3).

10/03/80 San Diego @ San Francisco Giants

Top of the 4th - Score 5-0 (two men on: Gene Tenace 1B, Luis Salazar 2B)
Putout Sequence: 4*-6*-3*

Dave Cash (SD) is the batter. He hits a line drive cleanly fielded by second baseman Guy Sularz (Out 1), Sularz throws to shortstop Joe Pettini who doubles up the runner caught off second base, Luis Salazar (Out 2), Pettini throws to Rich Murray, who catches the runner off first base, Gene Tenace (Out 3).

05/08/98 San Francisco Giants @ Chicago (N)

Bottom of the 4th - Score 0-2 (two men on: Henry Rodriguez 1B, Mark Grace 2B)
Putout Sequence: 3*-3*-6*

Jeff Blauser (CHI) is the batter with a 2-1 count. He hits a line drive to first baseman Charlie Hayes (Out 1), Hayes steps on the bag to nab the runner caught off first base, Henry Rodriguez (Out 2), Hayes throws over to shortstop Rich Aurilia, who tags the runner caught off second, Mark Grace (Out 3).

06/14/99 San Francisco Giants @ Colorado

Bottom of the 5th - Score 0-1 (two men on: Henry Blanco 1B, Angel Echevarria 2B)
Putout Sequence: 5*-4*-3*

Edgard Clemente (COL) is the batter. He hits a ground ball fielded by third baseman Bill Mueller who steps on the bag to force the runner from second base, Angel Echevarria, (Out 1), Mueller throws to second baseman Jeff Kent who forces the runner at second base, Henry Blanco (Out 2), Kent throws to J.T. Snow, who retires the batter, Edgard Clemente at first base (Out 3).

♦ Lost Home Runs

Through the years, many batters have hit home runs that do not appear as part of their batting record. Most of these apparent home runs were lost due to inclement weather conditions such as rain outs, and the statistics being erased. However, there have been quite a few four-baggers that have been ultimately credited as some other event in the record of the game, due to human error on the field. Base-runners and umpires account for most of these errors. Here is one instance where the umpire actually helped the Giants steal a win.

August 23, 1995 - San Francisco at New York (N)

At Shea Stadium, the Giants led 3-2 with two out in the bottom of the ninth inning with Chris Jones at bat for the Mets. Jones hit a drive to right field which appeared to be a game-tying home run off of Terry Mulholland. However, first base umpire Gary Darling ruled the ball foul. Replays clearly showed the ball hitting the fair pole, thus a game-tying home run. Forced to return to the plate and continue his at-bat, Jones was struck out by Mulholland on the very next pitch to end the game and preserve a complete game four-hitter for the Giant's lefty.

♦ Quick Facts / Did You Know?

"Say No"

Amazingly, great slugger Willie Mays never won a National League RBI title in his career.

"Teddy Coach"

Late in his career, legendary hitter Ted Williams served as mentor to young Willie McCovey when "Stretch" was arriving on the scene. Aside from various key tips provided by Ted, one of the most important related to the actual bat McCovey was using. Williams suggested that Willie switch from a 38 ounce bat to a 34 ounce bat to increase his bat speed. Both Hall-of-Famers finished their careers with 521 home runs.

A Different Hall

Willie Mays and Willie McCovey, among others, are members of the Ted Williams Hitters Hall-of-Fame.

A Win and a Save

On June 4, 2006, Jonathan Sanchez earned his first career win in the Giants' victory over the Mets at Shea Stadium. In the same game, Jeremy Accardo notched his first Major League save. This marked the second time that a San Francisco pitcher's first save came in a game in which another pitcher recorded his first career win. The other time it happened was April 18, 1970, when Mike McCormick, a veteran who was primarily a starter during his career, saved a victory for Jim Johnson.

Up Against a Wall

In the *Official Baseball Rules* (1978 and up), Rule 1.04 stipulates that any new park built shall have a minimum distance of 325 feet from home plate to the nearest fence (right or left fields). As you know, the right field wall at AT&T Park is just 309 feet. The Giants had to obtain special approval from Major League Baseball prior to the building of the park. The argument was that the landscape layout of the lot, would not allow for a fence to be built any further toward the bay.

Another First

In 1993, Sherry Davis became the first full-time female public address announcer in Major League history at Candlestick Park. Davis held the job for seven seasons.

Willie's Last Hit Ever

Although Willie Mays' last career hit occurred in a New York Mets uniform, it should still be cited. The final hit of Willie's spectacular career drove in a run in the 12th inning of Game 2 of the 1973 World Series at Oakland. The Mets won that game 10-7, but lost the Series.

Peter Magowan, Owner

Like Bob Lurie before him, Peter Magowan was hailed as a white knight when he saved the team from leaving San Francisco in 1993. Magowan put together a conglomerate that purchased the team. Magowan was a life long Giants fan. Born in New York, he idolized Willie Mays and followed the team closely. Coincidentally, Magowan's family moved to the Bay Area about the same time the Giants did. Magowan was a well respected owner and executive of the game. He had a true sense of the history and heritage of the game. When Pacific Bell Park opened, he and his wife Debbie donated the statue of Willie Mays that now marks the entrance to the Park at Willie Mays Plaza.

Uniforms Throughout the Years

When the Giants arrived from New York, their uniforms, like the rest of the league, were conservative. They maintained that look until the styles of the 1970s changed around the Major Leagues. At that point, the switch went from traditional flannel or wool button down jerseys and belted pants to polyester pullover tops and beltless trousers. Color was also introduced, with orange and black becoming more prominent. In the mid- 1980s, the team returned to a more classic style, with button down tops and belted pants, with the traditional gray and white colors for road and home, respectively. In 1994, the club kept the classic look and returned to a more traditional name font, taken from their early days. When the club moved into Pacific Bell Park they unveiled a look that was characterized as a "traditional but modern theme." This reflected traditional uniforms from their past while incorporating modern accents. The one big difference was the use of cream color for home uniforms, rather than basic white. Briefly, during the 2001 season, the club had an all-black "alternate" jersey for Friday games only. All teams, including the Giants, have also adopted the "batting practice" jerseys and hats over the years. Here are some more specific wardrobe details.

1958

The only change was the cap logo which went from "NY" to "SF."

1973

The Giants changed their uniform for the first time since moving to San Francisco. This very slight modification was a reversal of the lettering colors, orange and black, on the names and numerals of both the home and road versions.

1977

This is when the pullover tops and beltless pants made a debut. The front of the new home uniform sported a new logo, now using a script version of "Giants" in orange and black. An alternate home jersey, in black, was occasionally worn, usually for the second game of a double-header. The road jerseys were orange and carried a block "San Francisco" on the front.

1978

The club made one minor change to the road jersey. The block "San Francisco" was switched to the script "Giants," as the home version had.

1983

The team discarded the pullover look for a more old-style, classic look. The uniform was once again a button-down jersey, belted pants and the basic colors of white for the home jersey and basic gray for the road. The home version had "Giants" in a new modern block form. The road version had an interlocking "SF."

1994

The Giants returned to an even more traditional "Giants" and "San Francisco" font for their uniform names and numerals. The font included chiseled serifs. The "SF" on the front of the road jersey was replaced with "San Francisco" once again.

2000

When opening the new park, the Giants decided to really go "old school" and eliminate players' names from the home jerseys. The home uniform changed from white to an older looking cream color. The team name font reverted back to the style that had been adopted in New York and carried to San Francisco. Accents to lettering included the addition of a thin line in gold.

2001

The organization added an alternate version of both the home and road uniform. This featured a black jersey and an alternate cap that had a raised "SF" monogram in black, outlined with orange piping. The black jerseys were an exact design to the regular home and road versions, except for the color change. The team wore the alternates on Fridays only. The team's regular pants were utilized with the black top. The alternate jerseys were discontinued after the 2002 season.

05/24/00: Shawn Estes: Complete Game Shutout and Grand Slam Home Run vs. Montreal

Shawn Estes had one of the most memorable all-around performances in Giant franchise history on May 24, 2000 against the Montreal Expos. Not only did Estes pitch a complete game shutout, but he also hit a grand slam home run en route to an 18-0 victory; in all, Estes had five runs batted in. His grand slam home run was the first in San Francisco team history for a pitcher and the first for the franchise since 1949. The win was the largest margin of victory in a shutout for the Giants since 1900.

Terrell Lowery: Spectacular Giants Debut and Stretch - May 2000

Terrell Lowery, an Oakland native, had played in over 750 career minor league games and had only about 100 Major League games to his credit when he made his Giant debut. Lowery was called up to the club in mid-May when Ellis Burks went on the disabled list. Lowery was on fire from his very first at-bat with the team, going 3-for-3, including a home run in his first game. In the coming weeks, his streak continued, as he batted a blazing .556 (15-27). This included a career high five-hit (three doubles) game at Milwaukee. The Giants could not find a place for him and he was sent back to AAA Fresno until the September expanded rosters (where he went 0-for-7, but still hit .441 for the year). It is amazing to note that Lowery batted *only* .199 in 84 minor league games. Lowery may be best remembered for his basketball prowess as point guard on the run and gun teams of Loyola Marymount University in the late '80s and early '90s; a teammate of the late Hank Gathers.

His 2000 line:

G	AVG.	AB	R	H	2B	3B	HR	RBI	BB	OB %
24	.441	34	13	15	4	0	1	5	7	.537

July 2000: Robb Nen Breaks Major League Baseball Save Record for Month

Robb Nen established a Major League record for most saves in the calendar month of July when he recorded his 14th in a 4-3 win versus Milwaukee on July 31, 2000. In that game, he worked a perfect 11th inning to save the victory. It marked his 13th straight save opportunity. Overall during the month, he was successful in 14 of 15 opportunities (only blown save 07/02 vs. Los Angeles). Statistically, he was 2-0 with a 0.60 earned-run average (one ER, 16.0 IP) and yielded a microscopic .075 batting average (4-for-75), issued only three walks and struck out 27

2000: National League Western Division Champions

The Giants won the National League Western Division title for the fifth time in their history. On the mound, the team was led by five starting pitchers that won 11 or more games, and Robb Nen's 41 saves; as a team, they were fourth in pitching in the National League. Offensively, the team was sparked by nine hitters with 10 or more home runs and four players that had 96 runs batted in, and tied for second in National

League team batting. Barry Bonds clubbed a then career-high 49 home runs, while teammate and National League MVP Jeff Kent had 125 runs batted in. As a team, they broke the franchise record for home runs with 226, bettering the old mark by five (1947).

Chapter 11: 2001-2003 - The Bonds Magic

04/18/01: Barry Bonds' 500th Career Home Run vs. Los Angeles

Barry Bonds became the 17th Major League player to hit 500 career home runs, and the first to do it with a splash. Bonds' two-run, eighth inning drive off Dodger Terry Adams went into San Francisco Bay and led the Giants over Los Angeles, 3-2. The home run off Adams splashed into McCovey Cove beyond the right field fence. Bonds rounded the bases and jumped with both feet on home plate before embracing his father, former Major Leaguer Bobby Bonds. The left field fence opened up and former Giants Willie Mays and Willie McCovey, also members of the 500 Home Rub Club, were whisked by a golf cart to a ceremony at home plate. Mays, Bonds' godfather, hit 660 home runs, McCovey 521. The crowd cheered deafeningly for every Bonds' at-bat, waved orange rally towels passed out before the game, and chanted "Barry! Barry!" Those in the outfield bleachers and along the top of the right field wall would rise in anticipation of each Bonds appearance. The walkway outside the wall edging McCovey Cove was packed with fans hoping to snag the historic number 500. The cove was filled with boats, and even a man in a wetsuit floating on a surfboard. Bonds was the first player to reach 500 home runs since Mark McGwire did it in 1999. The

36 year-old outfielder was the eighth quickest to hit 500, reaching it in 7,501 at-bats. McGwire did it the fastest, in 5,487 at-bats.

10/05, 07/01: Barry Bonds' Record Breaking 71st and 73rd Season Home Runs vs. Los Angeles

On October 5, Barry Bonds hit his 71st and 72nd home runs of the season to set a new Major League single-season record in the Giants' 11-10 heartbreaking loss to the Dodgers. The first inning blast to break the record came off Dodgers' pitcher Chan Ho Park. Bonds broke the mark set by Mark McGwire of 70 in 1998. The game took four hours, 27 minutes to complete, the longest nine-inning game in Major League history. With the Giants eliminated, Bonds did not start on Saturday (next day) but did bat once and contributed a pinch-hit single on the only good pitch he saw.

On October 7, the Giants beat the Dodgers 2-1 on the last day of the season, as Barry Bonds extended his Major League record with his 73rd home run of the season. He finished the campaign with a slugging percentage of .863 to break Babe Ruth's all-time single-season mark. Bonds had 411 total bases, third in the National League behind Luis Gonzalez and Sammy Sosa. He also became the only player besides Yankee Kevin Maas to have more than 20 home runs and not double his home run total in RBI. (Maas had 21 home runs, 41 RBI, in 1991).

Summary by Home Run

#	Date	Pitcher	Opponent	Inning	Distance
I	04/02	Woody Williams	San Diego	5th	420' LCF
2	04/12	Adam Eaton	@ San Diego	4th	417' RCF
3	04/13	Jamey Wright	@ Milwaukee	Ist	440' RCF
4	04/14	Jimmy Haynes	@ Milwaukee	5th	410' RF
5	04/15	David Weathers	Milwaukee	8th	390' LCF
6	04/17	Terry Adams	Los Angeles	8th	417' RF
7	04/18	Chan Ho Park	Los Angeles	7th	420' RCF

8	04/20	Jimmy Haynes	Milwaukee	4th	410' LCF
9	04/24	Jim Brower	Cincinnati	3rd	380' RCF
10	04/26	Scott Sullivan	Cincinnati	8th	430' CF
11	04/29	Manny Aybar	Chicago	4th	370' RF
12	05/02	Todd Ritchie	@ Pittsburgh	5th	420' LCF
13	05/03	Jimmy Anderson	@ Pittsburgh	1st	420' LCF
14	05/04	Bruce Chen	@ Philadelphia	6th	360' RF
15	05/11	Steve Trachsel	New York	4th	410' RCF
16	05/17	Chuck Smith	@ Florida	3rd	420' RCF
17	05/18	Mike Remlinger	@ Atlanta	8th	391' RF
18	05/19	Odalis Perez	@ Atlanta	3rd	416' RCF
19	05/19	Jose Cabrera	@ Atlanta	7th	440' RCF
20	05/19	Jason Marquis	@ Atlanta	8th	410' LCF
21	05/20	John Burkett	@ Atlanta	1st	415' CF
22	05/20	Mike Remlinger	@ Atlanta	7th	436' CF
23	05/21	Curt Schilling	@ Arizona	4th	430' CF
24	05/22	Russ Springer	@ Arizona	9th	410' LCF
25	05/24	John Thomson	Colorado	3rd	400' RF
26	05/27	Denny Neagle	Colorado	1st	390' RF
27	05/30	Robert Ellis	Arizona	2nd	420' RF
28	05/30	Robert Ellis	Arizona	6th	410' CF
29	06/01	Shawn Chacon	@ Colorado	3rd	420' RF
30	06/04	Bobby Jones	San Diego	4th	410' CF
31	06/05	Wascar Serrano	San Diego	3rd	410' LCF
32	06/07	Brian Lawrence	San Diego	7th	450' CF
33	06/12	Pat Rapp	Anaheim	1st	320' RF
34	06/14	Lou Pote	Anaheim	6th	430' RCF
35	06/15	Mark Mulder	Oakland	1st	380' LCF
36	06/15	Mark Mulder	Oakland	6th	430' RCF
37	06/19	Adam Eaton	@ San Diego	5th	375' RCF
38	06/20	Rodney Myers	@ San Diego	8th	347' RF
39	06/23	Darryl Kile	@ St. Louis	1st	380' RF
40	07/12	Paul Abbott	@ Seattle	1st	429' RCF

41	07/18	Mike Hampton	Colorado	4th	320' RF
42	07/18	Mike Hampton	Colorado	5th	360' LF
43	07/26	Curt Schilling	@ Arizona	4th	375' RF
44	07/26	Curt Schilling	@ Arizona	5th	370' LCF
45	07/27	Brian Anderson	@ Arizona	4th	440' RF
46	08/01	Joe Beimel	Pittsburgh	1st	400' RCF
47	08/04	Nelson Figueroa	Philadelphia	6th	405' RF
48	08/07	Danny Graves	@ Cincinnati	11th	430' RCF
49	08/09	Scott Winchester	@ Cincinnati	3rd	350' RF
50	08/11	Joe Borowski	@ Chicago	2nd	396' CF
51	08/14	Ricky Bones	Florida	6th	410' RF
52	08/16	A.J. Burnett	Florida	4th	380' RF
53	08/16	Vic Darensbourg	Florida	8th	430' RCF
54	08/18	Jason Marquis	Atlanta	8th	415' RCF
55	08/23	Graeme Lloyd	@ Montreal	9th	380' RCF
56	08/27	Kevin Appier	@ New York	5th	375' RCF
57	08/31	John Thomson	Colorado	8th	400' RF
58	09/03	Jason Jennings	Colorado	4th	435' RCF
59	09/04	Miguel Batista	Arizona	7th	420' RCF
60	09/06	Albie Lopez	Arizona	2nd	420' RCF
61	09/09	Scott Elarton	@ Colorado	1st	488' RCF
62	09/09	Scott Elarton	@ Colorado	5th	361' RF
63	09/-09	Todd Belitz	@ Colorado	11th	394' RCF
64	09/20	Wade Miller	Houston	5th	410' CF
65	09/23	Jason Middlebrook	@ San Diego	2nd	411' CF
66	09/23	Jason Middlebrook	@ San Diego	4th	365' LF
67	09/24	James Baldwin	@ Los Angeles	7th	360' RF
68	09/28	Jason Middlebrook	San Diego	2nd	440' RCF
69	09/29	Chuck McElroy	San Diego	6th	435' RF
70	10/04	Wilfredo Rodriguez	@ Houston	9th	480' RCF
71	10/05	Chan Ho Park	Los Angeles	1st	440' RCF
72	10/05	Chan Ho Park	Los Angeles	3rd	410' CF
73	10/07	Dennis Springer	Los Angeles	1st	380' RF

Bonds' Home Runs Breakdown by the Numbers

Day of the Week

Sunday: 11
Monday: 6
Tuesday: 9
Wednesday: 8
Thursday: 17
Friday: 13
Saturday: 9

Month

April: 11
May: 17
June: 11
July: 6
August: 12
September: 12
October: 4

McCovey Cove "Splash Hit:" 9

Field Location

Left Field: 2
Left Center Field: 9
Center Field: 12
Right Center Field: 25
Right Field: 25

Number of Outs

0 Out: 21
1 Out: 29
2 Outs: 23

Number Runners on Base

0 On: 46
1 On: 21
2 On: 4
3 On: 2

By Inning

1st: 12
2nd: 5
3rd: 8
4th: 12
5th: 9
6th: 7
7th: 6
8th: 9
9th: 3
Extra: 2

Batting Pitch Count

0-0: 11
0-1: 5
0-2: 2
1-0: 7
1-1: 11
1-2: 1
2-0: 7
2-1: 8
2-2: 7
3-0: 2
3-1: 6
3-2: 6
After 1-0: 23
After 0-1: 39

Batting Lineup Location

3rd: 66

4th: 6

6th: 0

8th: 0

9th: 1

As Designated Hitter: 1

As Pinch-Hitter: 1

Miscellaneous Situations

vs. Right-Handed Pitchers: 56

vs. Left-Handed Pitchers: 17

Home: 37

Road: 36

Before All-Star Break: 39

After All-Star Break: 34

400+ Feet or More Distance: 47

Less Than 400 Feet Distance: 26

Single Home Run Games: 51

Multiple Home Run Games: 10

Day: 26

Night: 47

Grass: 71

Artificial Turf: 2

In Innings 1 - 6: 53

In Innings 7 +: 20

2001: Bonds and Aurilia - Second Most Single Season Home Runs by Teammate Duos in History (110)

There have been many, many teammates that have played together over the history of baseball that have proven to be prolific home run hitting duos. Willie Mays and Willie McCovey are two San Francisco Giants that fit that category. During the memorable 2001 season in which Barry Bonds broke the single-season home run mark with his 73 round trippers, when combined with Rich Aurilia's 37, the pair hit what is currently the second most by two teammates in history. Besides being second most, the pair also became only the fourth to break the century mark. Mark McGwire and Ray Lankford approached the record in McGwire's assault on Roger Maris' record in 1998. Here is a summary of the all-time twosome list:

Duo HR Total	Players	Team	Year
115	Maris (61) and Mantle (54)	Yankees	1961
110	**Bonds (73) and Aurilia (37)**	**Giants**	**2001**
107	Ruth (60) and Gehrig (47)	Yankees	1927
101	McGwire (70) and Lankford (31)	Cardinals	1998

Bonds and Aurilia hit back-to-back home runs seven times during the season. This is one short of the all-time record set in 1997 by Andres Galarraga and Larry Walker of the Colorado Rockies.

2001: Jeff Kent and Rich Aurilia - First Middle Infield Duo to Hit 20 Home Runs in Three Consecutive Seasons in Major League History

In 2001, Jeff Kent (second base) and Rich Aurilia (shortstop) became the first duo in Major League Baseball history to hit 20 or more home runs in three consecutive seasons. Surprisingly, in 2000, they became just the first twosome to do it in consecutive years. Over the three-year span, Kent and Aurilia had some marvelous offensive campaigns that were highlighted by career years for each (Kent, '00 / Aurilia '01). Bobby Doerr and Vern Stephens of the Boston Red Sox were only other 2B / SS duo to have 20 clouts in same season twice having done so in 1948 and again in 1950.

	1999	2000	2001
Kent	23	33	22
Aurilia	22	20	37

Barry Bonds: 2001 Highest Season Slugging Average in History

During his monster, record-breaking season of 2001, Barry Bonds boasted an .863 slugging percentage. The old record, set by Babe Ruth 81 years before in 1920, was .847. Bonds bested it by a difference of .016 points or nearly two percent. Only Ruth in 1920 and 1921 had ever slugged over .800. The old National League record was .756 by Rogers Hornsby in 1925.

Barry Bonds: 2001 Magical Record Breaking Season

Where do you start and what else can be said? Barry Bonds arguably had the best offensive season ever by a Major League player. If it was not the best, it certainly was within the top three. His numbers and marks were Ruthian in nature, as he rivaled The Babe in many offensive categories. Here is a summary of just some of the achievements Bonds amassed:

♦ Hit 73 home runs to break Mark McGwire's single-season Major League record (1998).
♦ Set Major League record for most home runs on the road in a season with 36.
♦ His 10 multiple home run games were good for second all-time, behind Hank Greenberg (1938) and Sammy Sosa (1998) who each clubbed 11.
♦ Finished with a slugging percentage of .863, surpassing the Major League record of .847 set by Babe Ruth in 1920.
♦ Walked 177 times, breaking Ruth's Major League record of 170 set in 1923.
♦ Hit a home run every 6.52 at-bats, breaking the Major League record of one per 7.27 at-bats set by McGwire in 1998.
♦ Finished with an on-base percentage of .515, the best in the Major Leagues since 1957, and tops in the National League since John McGraw's mark of .547 in 1899.

♦ Hit his 500th career home run on April 17 against Los Angeles.

♦ Set career high with 137 runs batted in.

♦ Hit a home run in a career-high six straight games, including his 500th home run on April 17. Bonds was the 17th Major Leaguer to reach the milestone.

♦ Had another six-game home run streak in mid-May, setting a National League record with nine home runs in that span. He also tied a record by hitting a home run in four straight official at-bats.

♦ Connected for a home run twice on May 30, becoming the most prolific left-handed home run hitter in National League history with number 522. That moved him past Hall-of-Famers Willie McCovey and Ted Williams on the all-time list.

♦ Had a Major League record 17 home runs in May, and stayed just as hot in early June. He got halfway to McGwire's mark by hitting his 35th and 36th home runs in mid-June. Bonds passed the month's record of 15 hit by the Yankee's Mickey Mantle in 1956 and the Cardinal's Mark McGwire in 1998. The 17 roundtrippers also tied the Major League mark for most by a left-handed hitter in any month (Babe Ruth NY (A), September, 1927).

♦ Posted 107 extra-base hits for third highest total in Major League history, tying Chuck Klein's National League mark set in 1930.

♦ Became the oldest player in Major League history to reach 50 home run plateau with blast August 11 at Chicago (off Joe Borowski), as he was 37 years and 18 days of age.

♦ Had greatest first-half power numbers in Major League history, blasting record 39 home runs before the All-Star break; the old mark of 37 clouts was established by Reggie Jackson in '69 and Mark McGwire in '98.

Barry Bonds: 2001 National League Most Valuable Player

Barry Bonds capped a season of shattered records and was named the National League's Most Valuable Player for 2001. Bonds, who hit 73 home runs to become the new single-season home run king, became baseball's first four-time Most Valuable Player, winning the award by a wide margin of votes by the Baseball Writers' Association of America. Bonds was first on 30 of 32 ballots and was second on the other two ballots to finish with 438 points. Barry easily outdistanced runner-up Sammy Sosa. Bonds had previously won the award in 1993 with San Francisco and in 1992 and 1990 with the Pittsburgh Pirates. At this point, he stood alone as a four-time MVP, surpassing three-time winners Stan Musial, Roy Campanella and Mike Schmidt in the National League; and Jimmie Foxx, Joe DiMaggio, Yogi Berra and Mickey Mantle in the American League. Bonds has twice finished second in MVP voting, including in 2000 to Giants' teammate Jeff Kent. In addition to breaking Mark McGwire's season record of 70 home runs set in 1998, Bonds batted .328 with 137 runs batted in while shattering two other Major League records long held by the legendary Babe Ruth. Bonds' 177 walks surpassed Ruth's 170 in 1923 and his .863 slugging percentage was higher than Ruth's .847 in 1920.

08/09/02: Barry Bonds' 600th Career Home Run vs. Pittsburgh

Barry Bonds hit the 600th home run of his career against the Pirates and joined the select company of Hank Aaron, Babe Ruth, and Willie Mays (his godfather) in the exclusive club. Barry hit the historic home run capping an amazing two-year power surge by becoming the fourth Major Leaguer to reach the lofty mark, and the first to do it in 31 years. The blast off Kip Wells was a 421 foot solo shot to center field in the sixth inning. No player had crossed the threshold since Aaron did it in April, 1971.

San Francisco Giants All-Time Retired Uniform Numbers

Over their 50 years in San Francisco, the Giants have retired the uniform number of just five select players. They are all inducted in the Hall-of-Fame in Cooperstown. Surely coming as no surprise, the players are: Willie Mays, Juan Marichal, Willie McCovey, Orlando Cepeda and Gaylord Perry.

#	Player Giant's Years	San Francisco Highlights
24	**Willie Mays** 1958 - 72	◆ Leader in Most Giant Offensive Categories ◆ 1979 Hall-of-Fame
27	**Juan Marichal** 1960 - 73	◆ Leader in Most SF Pitching Categories ◆ No-Hitter in 1963 ◆ 1983 Hall-of-Fame
30	**Orlando Cepeda** 1958 - 66	◆ 1958 N. L. Rookie of the Year ◆ 1999 Hall-of-Fame
36	**Gaylord Perry** 1962 - 71	◆ 134 Wins in SF ◆ No Hitter in 1968 ◆ 1991 Hall-of-Fame
44	**Willie McCovey** 1959 - 73 1977 - 80	◆ 1959 N. L. Rookie of the Year ◆ Leader in Most SF Offensive Categories ◆ 1986 Hall-of-Fame

San Francisco Giants All-Time Hall-of-Fame Inductees

Over their 50 years in San Francisco, the Giants have been blessed with the spectacular play of many individuals. A very exclusive number have been inducted into the Hall-of-Fame. No surprise, the players are: Willie Mays, Juan Marichal, Willie McCovey, Gaylord Perry and Orlando Cepeda.

Player Year Enshrined Position	Career Highlights
Willie Mays *1979* Center Field	♦ 660 Home Runs (4th Most) ♦ 12-Time Gold Glove winner ♦ 24 All-Star Games ♦ 1965 N. L. MVP ♦ MLB All-Century Team
Juan Marichal *1983* Pitcher	♦ 9 All-Star Games ♦ 0.50 ERA in All-Star Games ♦ 20 Wins / 6 Times - 238 in SF
Willie McCovey *1986* 1st Base / LF	♦ 6 All-Star Games ♦ 521 Home Runs ♦ 18 Grand Slams (N. L. Record) ♦ 1969 N. L. MVP
Gaylord Perry *1991* Pitcher	♦ 5 All-Star Games ♦ 2 Cy Young Awards (not w/ SF) ♦ 20 Wins / 5 Times - 2 in SF ♦ Over 300 Wins - 134 in SF
Orlando Cepeda *1999* 1st Base / RF	♦ 1958 N. L. Rookie of the Year ♦ 6 All-Star Games ♦ 1 N. L. MVP Award

In addition, the following members of the Hall-of-Fame played with the San Francisco Giants during their career:

Player Year Enshrined Position	Giant's Year(s)
Warren Spahn 1973 Pitcher	1965
Duke Snider 1980 Outfield	1964
Joe Morgan 1990 2nd Base	1981 - 82
Steve Carlton 1994 Pitcher	1986
Gary Carter 2003 Catcher	1990

2002 National League Wild Card and National League Champions

For the second consecutive season, the Giants fell just a couple of games short of the division leading Arizona Diamondbacks. However, they qualified for the playoffs as the National League Wild Card Champion. Barry Bonds had another monster offensive season and newcomers David Bell (20 HR), Kenny Lofton and Reggie Sanders (85 RBI) were plugged into a lineup that already had strong veterans like Jeff Kent (37 HR / 108 RBI) and Rich Aurilia. The pitching staff was supported by five starters that won 12 games or more: Russ Ortiz (14), Kirk Rueter (14), Ryan Jensen (13), Jason Schmidt (13) and Livan Hernandez (12). Felix Rodriguez and Tim Worrell were unstoppable set-up men in the seventh and eighth innings for closer Robb Nen (43 saves). Manager

Dusty Baker pulled all of the right strings as the Giants were National League Champions for the first time since 1989.

2002 National League Divisional Playoff Series vs. Atlanta

The perennial playoff team of the 1990s, the Atlanta Braves, posed a formidable threat to the Giants. The vaunted pitching staff of the Braves made the Giants a sure underdog in the five-game series. Kenny Lofton, a late-season acquisition, put on a tremendous performance by setting the table and getting on base for the team's power hitters. Russ Ortiz anchored the pitching staff and won the important first and fifth games of the series. The Giants forced a decisive Game 5 on the arm of Livan Hernandez, who gave a gutsy 8 1/3 inning performance in Game 4, as the Giants scored seven runs in the first three innings and won 8-3. Rich Aurilia made an incredible game saving play in Game 5 that preserved the lead and the win.

2002 National League Championship Series vs. St. Louis

Veteran catcher Benito Santiago was named the National League Championship Series Most Valuable Player following the Giants' 2-1 victory over the St. Louis Cardinals in Game 5. The sweetest reward was the spot the team earned in the World Series. Santiago hit .300 with two home runs and six runs batted in against the Cardinals in five games, highlighted by his two-run home run in the eighth inning that provided the winning run in Game 4. Though he failed to make a big play in three clutch situations during Game 5, he was still the star of the series. The Giants wrapped up the series with a dramatic bottom of the ninth win in Game 5. Kenny Lofton smashed the first pitch from Steve Kline into right field to score David Bell from second base and send the team to the World Series. The bullpen came through again for the Giants throughout the five games, with Tim Worrell picking up two wins and Robb Nen earning three saves. Bell hit .412 for the series and Aurilia had five runs batted in.

Barry Bonds: All-Time Record for Walks / Intentional Walks / On-Base % In Season - 2002, Part I

After his incredible 2001 season, National League managers searched for ways to try to neutralize Barry Bonds at the plate. Bonds was in the midst of one of the most dominant grooves as any hitter to ever play the game. Pitchers learned that Bonds could reach and pummel pitches no matter what the location was, inside, outside, high or low. Bonds was able to reach these pitches with power and send them flying out of ballparks. Managers had no choice but to intentionally walk Barry and try to diminish, or at least minimize, his impact.

During the record-setting 73 home run campaign of 2001, Bonds set a new Major League record for walks in a season with 177. The 2002 season saw him break his own record and walk a stunning 198 times. Sixty-eight of those walks were intentional passes. The 68 intentional walks blew past the previous record set by another Giant, the most feared power hitter of his era, Willie McCovey, in his MVP season of 1969 (45).

The excessive number of walks allowed Bonds to keep his batting average up when he was able to finally put the ball in play, well up over the .350 mark. Bonds ended the season as the National League batting champion at .370. Another byproduct of the increased number of walks was Bonds' on-base percentage. The mark of .582 was the highest in the National League in over 100 years and the best in Major League Baseball in over 40 years.

Barry Bonds: Most Intentional Walks in Major League History

Barry Bonds was made in the mold of his father Bobby, with a combination of power and speed. Like his dad, Bonds became a member of the exclusive 30-30 club on multiple occasions. As aforementioned, because of his power, Bonds was consistently walked intentionally by National League pitchers. Early in the 1999 season, Bonds received his 294th intentional pass, passing Hank Aaron for the Major League record. Bonds was even walked intentionally once with the bases loaded in the bottom of the ninth inning. Arizona Diamondback manager Buck Showalter made the decision he did not want to give Bonds the opportunity to end the game with his bat. Each time the catcher puts up four fingers and Bonds drops the bat and armor and heads to first base, he adds to his own record.

Barry Bonds: Continues the Magic in 2002

How do you top 2001? Barry Bonds followed up his monumental 2001 campaign with a memorable season in 2002. He continued his absolute dominance of the league with astounding numbers. Here is a summary of just some of the achievements Bonds amassed:

- ♦ Won first National League batting title at .370, while leading the Major Leagues, as well. Bonds was also the first San Francisco Giant to ever win the batting crown.
- ♦ Establishing Major League single-season records for on-base percentage (.582), walks (198) and intentional walks (68).
- ♦ Had an amazing postseason National League Division Series, National League Championship Series and World Series, hitting a combined .356 (16-45) with 18 runs, two doubles, one triple, eight home runs, 16 runs batted in, 27 walks, .a 978 slugging percentage and .581 on-base percentage.
- ♦ Eclipsed own all-time season walk record of 177, which he established in 2001, with an unbelievable new mark of 198.

- Shattered Willie McCovey's single-season intentional walk record of 45, which was set in 1969, with a new record of 68.
- Marked his 11th consecutive season with 30 home runs or more to extend his National League record.
- Had nearly as many home runs (46) as he did strikeouts (47). The last player to have more home runs (minimum of 10) than strikeouts in a season was Kansas City's George Brett in 1980 (24 HR, 22 strikeouts).
- Other offensive departments Bonds ranked among National League leaders were: runs (117 - 3rd), RBI (110 - T6th), slugging percentage (.799 - 1st), extra-base hits (79 - T3rd), RBI-ratio (1 every 3.7 at-bats - 1st) and HR-ratio (one every 8.8 at-bats - 1st)
- Was issued at least one walk in each of his last 18 games (34 walks total during span which began September 9), which set a National League record (former circuit mark of 16 straight games was established by St. Louis' Jack Clark in 1987 and Atlanta's Chipper Jones in 1999). The Major League standard is 22 straight contests with a walk set by Detroit's Roy Cullenbine in 1947. Bonds was walked a career-high five times September 12 in San Diego (one intentional), falling one shy of the Major League record for most free passes received in an extra-inning game (set by Cleveland's Andre Thornton, May 2, 1984 and Houston's Jeff Bagwell, August 20, 1999).
- Slugged 600th career home run August 9 against the Pittsburgh Pirates, a solo shot to centerfield off Kip Wells in sixth inning (estimated distance of 421 feet).
- Named as National League Player of the Month for August, marking his 10th player of month award in career. Since the award was established in 1958, no other player has won more than six times. In August, hit .447 (34-76) with 24 runs, six doubles, 11 home runs, 25 runs batted in, 37 walks (11 intentional), one stolen base, .961 slugging percentage and .621 on-base percentage.
- Slugged 43rd clout of year September 9 versus the Los Angeles Dodgers (off Odalis Perez). The blast that went an estimated

491 feet to straight-away centerfield at Pacific Bell Park and was the longest recorded at the Giants' new home and second longest of Bonds' career (earlier in campaign blasted 492-foot clout in Denver).

♦ Produced his fourth three-home run game of career and 24th four-hit game August 27th in Denver, finishing 4-for-4 with a double, three home runs, three runs batted in, one walk and four runs. It was his second three-home run game at Coors Field, having also accomplished the feat September 9, 2001.

♦ Clubbed 589th career home run June 12 in Toronto (in ninth inning off Cliff Politte), marking the 28th Major League ballpark he has hit home run in during regular season.

♦ Participated in MLB-Japan All-Star Series following the season, hitting .367 (11-for-30) with six runs, two doubles, five home runs and 12 runs batted in eight games.

Barry Bonds: 2002 National League Most Valuable Player

Barry Bonds added to his legend by responding to his paramount 2001 season with another record Most Valuable Player award. Barry won the National League batting title with a .370 average, slugged 46 home runs and had 110 runs batted in. Bonds was a unanimous selection, gaining all 32 first-place votes. He outdistanced runner-up Albert Pujols by a wide margin. Bonds previously won the award in '90, '92, '93 and '01. He extended his record of standing alone as a five-time MVP. Bonds catapulted himself into award contention by continuing to rewrite the record book and establishing Major League single-season records for on-base percentage (.582), walks (198) and intentional walks (68). Bonds also eclipsed his own season walk record of 177, which he set in 2001. Barry absolutely shattered Willie McCovey's intentional free pass mark of 45, which was set in 1969.

Dusty Baker, Manager

In 1993, the Giants were acquired by new ownership. The new group decided to bring in a new manager, a man who had previously been a player with the team, Dusty Baker. Over the next several years, Dusty demonstrated that he was truly one of the great tacticians of the game. Baker led that 1993 team to a San Francisco record 103 wins. He also led the team to the Western Division title in 1997. One of the most popular managers in team history, Baker had an extremely keen knack for communicating with players. Dusty ended with a career record of 840-715 (.540) with the Giants.

2002 World Series vs. Anaheim

All throughout the Series, the Giants bullpen provided solid support and kept the team in just about every game. The Angels tried to shut down Barry Bonds, but when he did get a chance to hit, he was able to continue his power surge with a .471 batting average and four home runs for the Series. The Giants took a 3-2 Series lead with a commanding 16-4 victory in Game 5 at Pacific Bell Park. The horizon looked rosy as the packed their bags for the short trip back to Anaheim.

Then, some may say that it was a Disney-like story ending. Whether it was or not, it certainly was a major disappointment for the Giants and their fans, once again. The Halos won the decisive Game 7 of the 2002 World Series, 4-1, over the Giants, to become the champions of Major League Baseball. The Giants held a 3-2 series lead, entering Game 6 in Anaheim, and a commanding 5-0 lead in the seventh inning. The Giants were a mere eight outs away from slamming the door for their first World Title in almost 50 years for the franchise and first in San Francisco. The momentum suddenly turned and they dropped that game and the last. The Angels rallied to score three runs in the seventh on Scott Spiezio's clutch, Series-turning home run. They added three more in the eighth on a Darin Erstad home run and a Troy Glaus two-run double. The series was even at 3-3, forcing Sunday's seventh game. The Giants held an early 1-0 lead, but could not muster any more offense, and fell 4-1.

Barry: 2002 All-Time Postseason Records
Established / Dominant Postseason

Although the Giants lost the World Series to the Angels in seven games, Barry Bonds demonstrated the offensive dominance that National League pitchers have long known. Bonds gave memorable performances in his first career World Series appearance. Despite the Angels effort to neutralize Bonds' impact with intentional walks, he still had a strong influence on the Giants offensive attack. Bonds hit one of the longest home runs in the history of Anaheim Stadium with a 430 foot plus blast in Game 1 off Jarrod Washburn. He became just the 26th player to hit a home run in their first World Series at-bat when he drilled a second-inning shot off Jarrod Washburn in Game 1 at Anaheim. Bonds established the all-time record for home runs in a single postseason with eight roundtrippers (three in LDS, one in LCS and four in WS). He also shattered the single postseason walk mark with 27, eclipsing Gary Sheffield's 1997 total of 20. A review of Bonds' postseason performance and records set or tied:

Series	AVG.	AB	R	H	2B	3B	HR	RBI	BB
NLDS	.294	17	5	5	0	0	3	4	4
NLCS	.273	11	5	3	0	1	1	6	10
World	.471	17	8	8	2	0	4	6	13
Totals	.356	45	18	16	2	1	8	16	27

Records Set

Most walks, Series - 13
Most intentional walks, game - 3, Game 4, 10/23/02
Most intentional walks, Series - 7
Highest on-base percentage, Series of more than 4 games - .700
Highest slugging percentage, Series of more than 4 games - 1.294

Records Tied

Most intentional walks, career - 7
Most runs scored, Series - 8
Most home runs, 7-game Series - 4
Most consecutive games, start of Series, home run - 3

2003 Website Fan Vote for the 1950s, 1960s, 1970s, 1980s and 1990s

San Francisco Giant All-Time "Classic Memories"

Throughout the 2003 season, Giants' fans were given the opportunity to vote for one Classic Giants Memory from each decade from the '50s through the '90s. The five winning selections are enshrined on a monument at China Basin Park. The top choices included a first glimpse of Hall-of-Fame stardom, a pair of National League Pennants and two moments that undoubtedly warmed the hearts of Giant's fans everywhere - downing the hated Dodgers in dramatic fashion. The winners for each decade:

1950s

"A Star is Born" Willie McCovey goes 4-for-4 in Major League Debut
July 30, 1959, at Seals Stadium (Giants vs. Phillies)

1960s

"A Giant Rally" San Francisco's First Pennant
October 3, 1962, at Dodger Stadium (Giants at Dodgers)

1970s

"A Pinch of Ivie" Mike Ivie's Grand Slam Beats Los Angeles
May 28, 1978, at Candlestick Park (Giants vs. Dodgers)

1980s

"27 Years of Waiting Have Come to an End" The Giants Win the 1989 National League Pennant
October 9, 1989, at Candlestick Park (Giants vs. Cubs in NLCS Game 5)

1990s

Rod Beck and Brian Johnson: "How the Giants Won the West"
September 18, 1997, at Candlestick Park (Giants vs. Dodgers)

Barry Bonds: First Player in Major League History to Hit 500 Home Runs and Steal 500 Bases for Career, Established in 2003

Giant great Barry Bonds added to his list of stellar career accomplishments in baseball history. On June 23, 2003, Barry stole his 500th career base versus the Los Angeles Dodgers. This was a key moment late in the game and helped the Giants go on to defeat the Dodgers. Earlier, in 2001, Bonds had hit his 500th career home run against the very same Dodgers on April 18. Bonds became the first player in Major League Baseball history to achieve this unique combination of power and speed. Bonds is also the only player ever to achieve the 400-400 level, as well.

2003 National League Western Division Champions

Most educated observers and fans were wondering how the Giants would even field a team, let alone be competitive for the 2003 season. Coming off of their World Series appearance, the Giants lost some one dozen players from the defending National League champion club, including key contributors Jeff Kent and Russ Ortiz. Brian Sabean and Ned Colletti wove their magic again and were able to retool the team to a high level of competitiveness. The team was again led by Bonds with 45 home runs and 90 runs batted in. Marquis Grissom came over and provided key offensive and defensive support in center field. When healthy, Ray Durham gave the Giants the leadoff hitter they coveted and Jose Cruz earned a Gold Glove in right field with his stellar defensive play. The pitching staff was led by the dominance of Jason Schmidt with 17 wins and a league-leading 2.34 earned-run average. The bullpen was strong with the surprising return of Joe Nathan (surgery) who amassed 12 wins in relief. Nen was lost for the year (surgery) but Tim Worrell assumed the role of closer and earned 45 saves. The Giants were only the ninth team in all of Major League history to lead the entire season from wire-to-wire (never out of first place). They won the division by an extraordinary 15 1/2 games after an absolutely torrid start that allowed them to sprint ahead of the division competition.

2003: National League Divisional Playoff Series vs. Florida

The Giants entered the National League Division Series on a high note. They faced the NL Wild Card Champion Florida Marlins in the first round, best-of-five series. True to form, they started the series in dominant fashion. Number one starter Jason Schmidt pitched a brilliant three-hit shutout, 2-0 on 109 pitches (89 strikes). After that, the series took a radical turn. In the middle of Game 2, the Giants surrendered a 4-1 lead in the fourth inning and never recovered the rest of the series. The defense that was such a strong element of the Giants' regular season success abandoned them in Games 3 and 4. The offense did not get timely hits and Florida took advantage by winning the last two games in their final at-bat, and the series three games to one. Edgardo Alfonzo was the only offensive highlight, hitting .556 (9-17) for the four-game series. The entire team was held without a home run for the series by a band of young Marlin pitchers that asserted their dominance.

Barry Bonds: 2003 National League Most Valuable Player

For an unparalleled third consecutive and sixth time overall, Barry Bonds was named the National League's Most Valuable Player for the 2003 season. Bonds' numbers may not have been as lofty as some of his previous efforts, but it was apparent that he still was the most dominant offensive force in the game. Bonds captured 28 of 32 first place votes in a race that was supposed to be a lot closer. During the season, many observers felt that Albert Pujols would be a runaway winner. To put Bonds' run in perspective, no other player in the entire history of Major League Baseball has more than three MVP awards total. For the year, Bonds posted a .341 batting average (third), hit 45 home runs (T-second), had 90 runs batted in, walked 148 times, had a .529 on-base percentage (first) and a .749 slugging percentage (first).

Rich Aurilia, Career

Solid play is the trademark of this professional. Rich Aurilia teamed with Jeff Kent to give the Giants strong support up the middle and at the plate for several seasons. Richie enjoyed his finest season in 2001 and emerged as one of the premier offensive shortstops in all of baseball. For his efforts, he was rewarded by being selected as a starter by the fans for the All-Star Game. For the year, he batted .324, hit 37 home runs and drove in 97, all career highs. Aurilia became just the third National League shortstop to ever hit 30 or more home runs in a single season (Banks-5x and Larkin -1x). His 206 hits also led the National League. This was the second most base-knocks in San Francisco history (Mays, 208, '58). Aurilia had a stellar postseason in 2002 as he shattered the Major League record for runs batted in by a shortstop with 17. He slugged the first inter-league grand slam home run versus Anaheim in 1997. Richie spent nine seasons with the Giants.

Willie Mays / Barry Bonds: Among Kings of the Multi-Home Run Games

Before his career is complete, Barry Bonds has an excellent chance of breaking another home run related record, multi-home run games. As of 08/25/06, Bonds has 68 multi- home runs games in his career. This mark puts Bonds in sole possession of second place on the all-time list. In 2004, he passed Mark McGwire, who had 67, for second. In late 2003, Bonds passed Willie Mays (63) and Hank Aaron (62) for sole possession of the third spot, at that time. Babe Ruth still holds the record at 72. Sammy Sosa, now retired, converged on the all-time leaders, checking in with 64.

Gang of Four: Barry Bonds / Willie Mays Among Top Four All-Time Home Run Kings

When Barry Bonds hit his 600th career home run in 2002, he became the first player to reach the ultra exclusive "600 Home Run Club" in over 30 years. The last player to reach the elite number was Hank Aaron who hit his 600th in April of 1971. He was well on his way to besting the all-time mark set by the legendary Babe Ruth in the early part of the century. Ruth hit his 600th home run in the summer of 1931 and ended up with a career total of 714. That was a record that stood for nearly 40 years. Willie Mays hit number 600 in 1969 and completed his fine career with 660 in 1973. Bonds reached his lofty target just a little over one year after passing the magical 500 home run mark. Each game Bonds played, he continued his assault on the record books. From the 2000 season forward, he joined the top of the elite in several major statistical categories. Dubbed "Mt. Crushmore" by the Giants, here is a detailed breakdown of the home run statistics of the mighty "Gang of Four."

Mt. Crushmore Roll Call (Elevation: 600 +)

Situation	Bonds	Mays	Ruth	Aaron
Career Home Runs	715	660	714	755
League Home Run Titles	2	4	12	4
30+ Home Run Seasons	14	5	2	7
40+ Home Run Seasons	8	4	7	8
50+ Home Run Seasons	1	2	4	0
60+ Home Run Seasons	1	0	1	0

Solo Home Runs	424	365	349	400
Two-Run Home Runs	207	219	251	245
Three-Run Home Runs	73	68	98	94
Grand Slam Home Runs	11	8	16	16
Multi Home Run Games	68	63	72	62
Home Runs: Home / Road	355 / 360	335 / 325	347 / 367	385 / 370
Home Runs vs. RHP / LHP	502 / 213	451 / 209	495 / 219	534 / 221
At-Bats Per Home Run	12.94	16.49	11.76	16.38
Home Runs Per 162 Games	41.8	35.6	46.2	37.1
Game Leadoff Home Runs	20	0	0	0
Pinch-Hit Home Runs	4	5	1	3
Inside-The-Park Home Runs	3	8	10	1
Extra-Inning Home Runs	11	22	16	14
Ballparks Hit Home Runs In	35	22	12	31
All-Star Game Home Runs	2	3	1	2
World Series Home Runs	4	0	15	3
# Pitchers Victimized For Home Runs	421	267	216	310
Best Home Run Season	73 ('01)	52 ('65)	60 ('27)	47 ('71)
# Seasons / Age at 600 Home Runs	16th / 38	18th / 38	18th / 36	18th / 37
# of Seasons Post 600 Home Runs	4	4	4	5

Bonds: As of hitting the 715th Home Run / Others: Career

04/12-13/04: Bonds Clobbers 660th and 661st Home Runs and Takes Sole Possession of Third Place on All-Time List

After an off-season of high anticipation and a week-long road trip to start the season, Barry Bonds came home to take the stage in his yard. Fans packed the park with eagerness to see him tie and then surpass all-time great slugger and godfather Willie Mays with his 660th and 661st home runs on April 12 and 13. On Opening Day at SBC Park, Bonds sent the crowd home happy by blasting a shot deep into McCovey Cove off of the Brewers' Matt Kinney. Willie Mays was on hand to officially "pass the torch" to Barry. Willie had the inscription on the torch he used in the 1996 Olympic Torch Run modified to celebrate Barry's accomplishment. Mays had traveled with the club for the entire week on the road in order to be present for the historic hit. The next night, Ben Ford was victimized as Bonds broke the record by smoking another shot into the Bay. Mays was present at that game, but did not come out on the field. This day there was no ceremony. No hugs. No torch. Oddly, the same fan secured **both** of the historic home run baseballs in McCovey Cove. Larry Ellison (not that Larry Ellison) braved the cold waters in his kayak and was lucky to pounce on both. Ellison immediately gave the 660th ball back to Bonds with little fanfare or publicity. He decided to keep the 661st ball for the time being, unsure of its future. Ahead for Bonds, he had only the immortal Babe Ruth and all-time king Hank Aaron in his sights.

04/12-20/04: Bonds Hits a Home Run in Seven Consecutive Games and Sets Record

Barry Bonds was on another of his absolute home run rampages during the team's first home stand of the 2004 season. True to his now legendary stature, Bonds provided excitement in every at-bat during the week. In addition to his record-breaking home run of note, he continued by settling in a power-stroking groove. On April 20, Bonds smashed a home run in his seventh straight game, bringing his career total to 667 at that point. The home run was only one shy of matching the Major League record for eight consecutive games with a home run, shared by Dale Long (Pittsburgh, 1956), Don Mattingly (New York (A), 1987) and Ken Griffey, Jr. (Seattle, 1993). Bonds set the National League record for total home runs in seven consecutive games with eight, thanks to a two-home run game during the streak. Barry hit a home run in the seven games in which he had an official at-bat. During the week of the streak, he had a pinch-hit walk which does not stop the streak under baseball's rules. Previously in his career, Bonds hit a home run in six straight games on two occasions, both during the 2001 season when he set the season record of 73 homers. He did it from April 12-18 and again from May 17-22. However, it was hard for Barry to enjoy this stretch because the Giants were marred by an early season slump of inconsistency at the plate, on the mound and in the field.

04/30/04: Brian Dallimore Grand Slam Home Run in First Major League Game / Hit

It is not often that 31-year-old rookies make it to the Major Leagues. It is even more rare for them to earn the spotlight right away. Former Stanford player Brian Dallimore did just that as he stole the show in his first Major League start, reaching base five times and scoring three runs. The big blow was Dallimore's grand slam home run that highlighted San Francisco's rally from an early seven-run deficit in the Giant's 12-9 victory over the defending World Champion Florida Marlins. He also hit two singles, drew a walk and got hit by a pitch. He joined the late Bobby Bonds as the only San Francisco Giants to blast a grand slam for their first hit. Dallimore, the 2003 PCL batting champion, was called up by the Giants after more than eight seasons (and more than 3,000 at-bats) in the minor leagues. His parents attended the game along with his wife and daughter, and they all joined the crowd in wild cheers as Dallimore pumped his fist while rounding the bases after his second-inning slam. Dallimore's dream of the big leagues was short-lived, as he spent just about two weeks with the team, before being returned to Fresno. He did resurface during the September roster expansion.

09/17/04: Barry Bonds Hits 700th Home Run vs. San Diego; only Third Man in Baseball History to Accomplish Earth-shattering Feat

It seems as if Barry Bonds was reaching significant home run levels just about every month. On September 20, 2004, he reached a plateau that had only been approached by two men in the entire history of the great game of baseball. Bonds crossed the threshold to immortality long ago, but he cemented his place even more on this day. Barry took an 0-1 curveball the opposite way off of the Padres' Jake Peavy in the third inning. He became just the third player to ever hit the monumental 700 mark. Of course, the only other men were Hank Aaron and Babe Ruth.

Barry Bonds: Runs Circles Around the Competition and Breaks Own All-Time Records for Walks / Intentional Walks / On-Base % in 2004 Season

The 2002 season for Barry Bonds was not describable in words. However, it could be categorized in with one significant one: "walk." As he progressed to an unrivaled and nearly mythical level of offensive performance at 40 years of age, the response by opposing managers during 2004 season can be described with two words: "obscenely fearful."

♦ Bonds' on-base percentage of .609 set a single-season record, breaking his own mark of .582 in 2002. His .609 OBA was 140 points higher than the second-place finisher (Colorado's Todd Helton at .469), and that margin between first and second place is also a record. The previous most lopsided victory was two years ago when Bonds (.582) finished 132 points ahead of

Pittsburgh's Brian Giles (.450). In the pre-Bonds era, the biggest margin of victory was 102 points in 1954 when Ted Williams (.513) squeaked past Minnie Minoso (.411) to win the American League on-base title. To put that in perspective, only one other current National Leaguer - Todd Helton - has ever had a season within 150 points of that. Bonds reached base 376 times. Only the Babe ever beat that.

♦ Bonds' 2004 slugging percentage was .812, fourth best all-time, and he joined Babe Ruth as the only players to have two slugging seasons of .800 or better. Bonds also outdistanced second-place Albert Pujols (.657) by 155 points. The last player, other than Bonds, to win a slugging title by at least 150 points was Ruth in 1926 when he slugged .737 to Al Simmons' .566.

♦ Bonds' record-setting 232 walks were a mammoth record 105 better than the three runners-up who had 127. The previous margin of victory was 72, when Ruth had 170 walks in 1923, and Joe Sewell had 98. The American League leader, Eric Chavez, did not even walk 100 times. Bonds was intentionally walked 120 times. No other team was within 50 of that. He walked so much that even if he'd gotten no hits all year, he still would have had a higher on-base percentage than the guy who led the league in hits, Juan Pierre.

♦ The average Major League player with 373 at-bats in 2004 (Bonds' total) had 33 walks. Therefore, Bonds finished 199 above the average, yet another record. One more astounding piece of trivia: Bonds' 232 walks were more than Shawon Dunston (5,927 at-bats), Manny Sanguillen (5,062 at-bats) or Ken Reitz (4,777 at-bats) had in their entire careers.

♦ Bonds had 120 intentional walks, breaking his own mark of 68 which he achieved in 2002. Philadelphia's Jim Thome finished second in the Major Leagues with 26 intentional walks. Bonds' margin of 94 more IBBs than the second-place finisher is a record. Bonds had more IBBs than any other team; the Cardinals were second with 64.

◆ Additionally, Barry became the oldest player in history to ever win a batting title at the age of 40. Bonds hit .362 for the year in 2004, his second crown in the past three seasons (.370, 2002).

Barry Bonds: 2004 National League Most Valuable Player, Record Seventh Award!

For a fourth consecutive and seventh time overall, Barry Bonds was named the National League's Most Valuable Player for 2004. He was the oldest to ever win the award. Some of Bonds' statistical numbers continued to defy logic and he continued his dominance of the National League. Bonds captured 24 of the 32 first place votes in the ballot. Although others like Adrian Beltre and Albert Pujols had breakout or career seasons, it became apparent during the season that Bonds would be the selection once again. To put Bonds' run in perspective, no other player in the entire history of Major League Baseball has more than three MVP awards total. For the year, Bonds posted a .362 batting average (second), hit 45 home runs (fourth), had 101 runs batted in, walked 232 times, had a .609 on-base percentage (first) and a .812 slugging average (first).

Bonds is the only player with more than three MVP awards and the only one to win more than two in a row. Willie Stargell was previously the oldest to win it, sharing the 1979 NL award with Keith Hernandez at 39 1/2. Among the four major North American professional sports, he trails only the NHL's Wayne Gretzky, who won nine MVPs. In the NBA, Kareem Abdul-Jabbar leads with six.

Seven MVP awards: That is more than Babe Ruth, Hank Aaron, Willie Mays and Ted Williams combined. Seven MVP awards: Over the last four decades, the Oakland A's are the only other team that has won that many. Seven MVP awards, just since 1990: In that same time, all the other players in the National League have only combined to win eight.

Most Base Hits in a Season by a Giants' Pitcher

The San Francisco Giants franchise has a tradition of excellent hitting pitchers. Back in the 1960s, Juan Marichal was one of the most dominant pitchers in the National League. He was also one of the best for that era with the bat, along with contemporaries like Don Drysdale and Bob Gibson. Juan posted four seasons of 20 hits or more: 28 (1966), 21 (1962), 20 (1963) and 20 (1968). The mark of 28 is a San Francisco record that still stands. Later into the '70s and '80s, pitchers like John Montefusco, Vida Blue, Renie Martin, Jim Gott and Don Robinson were respected hitters at the plate either. Gott is the last Giants' pitcher to hit two home runs in a game. He connected for the pair on May 12, 1985 against the Cardinals at Candlestick Park. In recent times, Livan Hernandez was the best hurler at the plate. Owning a career average over .240, Hernandez challenged Marichal's single-season hit total by gaining 21 hits in 2000 and 24 in 2001. In mid-summer 2001, Hernandez connected for a streak of eight consecutive base hits, finishing just two hits shy of the all-time National League record for any player, position or pitcher.

Robb Nen, Career

Robb Nen was one of the best in a long line of Giants' closers. He was also recognized as one of the preeminent closers in all of baseball during his period of dominance. Robb was the youngest pitcher to reach the 300-save plateau at 32 years of age. His 314 saves ranks 11th all-time. After joining the Giants in 1998, he amassed a franchise record 206 saves. When Nen saved 43 games in 2002, he became just the fourth pitcher in Major League history to have four separate 40-save seasons. Robb's seven consecutive 30-save seasons are second longest in history to only Trevor Hoffman's eight. Overall, Nen holds the second through sixth (tied) best San Francisco single-season save totals. Not letting anyone know, even his teammates, the gritty competitor held things together throughout the 2002 playoffs and World Series with a severely damaged shoulder and arm. This caused him to miss the entire 2003 and 2004 seasons. After three surgical procedures and several attempts to comeback, Nen announced his retirement just prior to the start of Spring Training 2005.

Nine Old Men: The 2005 Giants

The 2005 Giants achieved a record, of sorts, when their spikes touched the grass at SBC Park, at several times during the season. With Barry Bonds starting in left field, late in the season, the average age of San Francisco's everyday lineup was an amazing 35.875 years, the highest ever in Major League Baseball history. Baseball researcher John Korsgaard crunched the numbers and determined that this would have been a precedent to be set on Opening Day of the 2005 season.

With this in mind, the Giants could take heart in knowing that many other "older" clubs unearthed by Korsgaard during his research were highly successful. The 1945 Detroit Tigers, the first 20th century team with a lineup averaging 33 years of age, won the World Series. The 2001 Arizona Diamondbacks did the same with a lineup that also averaged 33. The 1983 Philadelphia Phillies, with an average age of 32, won the National League pennant. The '72 Tigers, the '82 California Angels and the '86 Angels each had a lineup averaging 32 and won division titles. However, the closest comparison to the Giants in terms of age is less promising. The 1998 Baltimore Orioles, whose lineup averaged 34 years, finished a below par 79-83 after winning their division just one year earlier. Manager Felipe Alou, at age 70, entered the '05 campaign as the second oldest manager in the game, as well. Bonds went on to miss most of the campaign, playing in just 14 late-season games. When he emerged in the lineup, history was almost made. Marquis Grissom (37) was no longer with then club and a much younger Randy Winn was starting in center field. Here is a list of how the Opening Day starting lineup would have looked:

Catcher: Mike Matheny, 34
1st Base: J.T. Snow, 37

2nd Base: Ray Durham, 33
Shortstop: Omar Vizquel, 37
3rd Base: Edgardo Alfonzo, 31
Left Field: Barry Bonds, 40
Center Field: Marquis Grissom, 37
Right Field: Moises Alou, 38

2005: Giants Honor Pitching Greats

The 2005 season was a year to pay tribute to three pitchers that have had a great impact on the Giant's success over the years.

Juan Marichal

The Giants dedicated a statue in honor of Juan Marichal. On May 21, the Giants unveiled the nine-foot bronze statue featuring Marichal's trademark high leg kick, in Lefty O'Doul Plaza. This is the entry gate first encountered by fans walking across the O'Doul Bridge across McCovey Cove. William Behrends, the sculptor who created the statues of Willie Mays and Willie McCovey, also crafted this statue of the "Dominican Dandy."

Gaylord Perry

The Giants' retired the number of Gaylord Perry (36) in a ceremony. Perry, the only San Francisco Giants Hall-of-Famer not to have his number retired by the organization, received that honor on July 23. Gaylord was inducted into the Hall-of-Fame in 1991 as a Giant, but he had become well known for wearing a jersey featuring the insignias of all his teams in legends and old-timers games. With this, Perry ended that practice, instead wearing a Giants' jersey at all such events.

Robb Nen

The Giants' acknowledged the career of recently retired closer Robb Nen. A pre-game ceremony was held on July 9. As a token of appreciation, the club presented Nen with a golf cart, complete with his trademark song "Smoke on the Water" that blows on the horn. Nen is the team's all-time saves leader (206). Robb's career ended abruptly after three shoulder operations for a torn rotator cuff. After injuring himself in 2002, he pitched throughout the playoffs and the World Series, showing extreme grit and determination. His last appearance was Game 6 in Anaheim. Nen missed the final two years of his contract (2003-04).

06/17/05: Tyler Walker Makes Relief Pitcher History at Detroit

In the ninth inning, the Tigers' Placido Polanco, Dmitri Young and Rondell White each singled to load the bases. Giants' manager Felipe Alou took out starting pitcher Jason Schmidt, and replaced him with closer Tyler Walker. Walker earned the save for his efforts, but his dominant performance goes far beyond, especially in the annals of relief history. Walker struck out three consecutive hitters, Ivan Rodriguez, Craig Monroe and Chris Shelton, all swinging, with the bases loaded. According to the Elias Sports Bureau, Walker made history by becoming the first pitcher to earn a save in that fashion since saves became an official statistic in 1969. Undoubtedly, some relievers have struck out the side with the bases loaded in non-save situations, and some pitchers of yesteryear must have done it to close out ballgames, but never had it occurred in the 37 years of the save era.

07/14/05: Giants Become First Team to Notch 10,000 Franchise Wins

It is entirely appropriate that the Giants' 10,000th win in franchise history was against the rival Los Angeles Dodgers at Chavez Ravine. The Giants became the first Major League Baseball team to reach the lofty plateau. In addition, they are the winningest team in North American professional sports history (10,000 - 8,511 on 07/14/05). The Giants needed almost 123 complete seasons to reach the distinguished milestone. It is also believed that the Giants are the first team in any sport, worldwide, to ever reach this position. The win was due to a hero not known for his home run power; Omar Vizquel belted a three-run shot, just his second of the season, in the seventh inning to power San Francisco into the victory column and the unique statistical category. The Giants won their first game on May 1, 1883, as the New York Gothams, with a 1-0 triumph over the Boston Beaneaters. Other milestone victories for the Giants while in San Francisco include:

Victory #	Date	Opponent	Score
7,000	07/18/68	St. Louis Cardinals	3-0
8,000	10/02/80	Los Angeles Dodgers	3-2
9,000	07/30/93	Colorado Rockies	10-4

Randy Winn, 2005: Wow, What a Trade Deadline Acquisition!

The Giants' anemic lineup was looking for some much needed power, speed and reliability the whole first half. In late July, at the trade deadline, they made a deal to obtain local product Randy Winn of San Ramon from the Mariners. In the two-plus months that he wore the Giants' uniform, the young center fielder was on fire at the plate and provided real boost to the offense. For the season, Winn batted .359, hit 14 home runs, and had 25 multi-hit games. That total included 11 games of three hits or more. Forty-one of his 83 hits were for extra bases.

In the last week of the season, the Giants slipped out of the playoff race, but Winn kept his offensive surge going. The center fielder led the National League with a .447 average in the month of September, including a torrid .556 over the final seven days of the season. For his efforts, Winn received the Bank of America National League Player of the Week award, as well as the Player of the Month honors. Winn recorded a league-best 15 hits and 29 total bases the last week, adding to his league-high 51 for the month. The 51 September hits were the most in one month by a Giants' player in at least 30 years. In September, his slugging percentage of .877 and 100 total bases led the circuit, and he was tied for the lead with 11 home runs. His final week average of .556 raised his Giants average to .359 in 58 games played.

His 2005 Giants line:

G	AB	R	H	2B	3B	HR	RBI	TB	BB	OB %	SLG %	AVG
58	231	39	83	22	5	14	26	157	11	.391	.680	.359

Selected Situational Batting Averages

September / October: .439
Leading-Off: .383
Ahead in Count: .474
First Inning: .442

J.T. Snow Career and Gold Gloves

The Giants have had a strong coverage at first base over the years. Names like McCovey and Clark come to mind. However, easily the best defensive first baseman they have ever had is J.T. Snow. After winning Gold Gloves for the California Angels in 1995 and 1996, Snow was traded to the Giants. He continued his slick fielding by winning Gold Gloves his first three years in the National League. He is one of just a handful of players to win multiple Gold Gloves in both leagues. Overall, he is fifth all-time in fielding his position. Snow was also productive with the bat, enjoying solid numbers at the plate during his career and delivering some memorable hits in key situations. In all, Snow spent nine seasons in a Giants' uniform.

Latin Legends Team: A True Honor
for Juan Marichal in 2005

San Francisco Giants' fans have always known that Juan Marichal was the greatest pitcher the franchise has ever seen. His career efforts have been documented in detail. In 2005, he was recognized on an even bigger stage for the true legend he was. In an effort to recognize the immense contributions that Latin players have had on the game of baseball, Major League Baseball initiated a program to select the "Latino Legends Team." More than 1.6 million votes were cast both online and at participating Chevrolet dealerships nationwide as part of the program. The winners were announced and introduced during a ceremony prior to Game 4 of the 2005 World Series at Minute Maid Park in Houston. Dodgers Hall-of-Fame Spanish broadcaster Jaime Jarrin began the ceremony by welcoming the fans, while actor Edward James Olmos introduced each player during the bilingual ceremony. Marichal was one of three starting pitchers named to the elite team. Juan also had the honor of throwing out the ceremonial first pitch for the game. In his 16-year career, Marichal compiled 243 wins and a 2.89 earned-run average. He started 451 games and completed 244 of them, pitching 52 shutouts. He was inducted into Cooperstown in 1983, the first player from the Dominican Republic to enter the Hall-of-Fame.

Sometimes, Legend is Transformed into Myth

Even amidst the true fabric of reality, a legendary figure or event can be transformed into myth. This happens over a period of time where the true facts become clouded or even somewhat forgotten and the witnesses no longer recollect with true accuracy. From 1951 to 1973, the great Willie Mays patrolled center field with adept prowess. There is no doubt that he was a legend of the game. In a 2000 television commercial for a major brewery, it was boasted that Willie Mays "threw out *hundreds* of runners at home plate" during his career. While this may seem like a truly realistic statistic, it is not the actual truth. The great minds at www.retrosheet.org investigate many items such as this. Actually, during his career, Mays had 195 assists as an outfielder. Through the current all-time box score update project, investigators have been able to document 143 of those assists. Willie threw out a grand total of 52 runners at home plate. Here is a breakdown of the rest of his assists:

Location	Number Gunned
1st Base	16
2nd Base	35
3rd Base	40

Spring 2006: Several Giants Participate in Inaugural World Baseball Classic

In March 2006, the world witnessed the first World Baseball Classic. This was a 16-nation tournament sanctioned by the International Baseball Federation (IBAF), and featured the best players competing for their home countries. This is the first time that a baseball event of this type was attempted to be organized. Major League players were eligible to compete in the 18-day event. The landmark field of countries invited included Australia, Canada, China, Cuba, the Dominican Republic, Italy, the Netherlands, Japan, Korea, Mexico, Panama, Puerto Rico, South Africa, Taiwan, the United States and Venezuela. The World Baseball Classic was a historic and unprecedented event. Several Giants players participated for their homelands. In all, they had six players take part. Barry Bonds would have been a seventh and key player for Team USA, but elected not to participate because of his injury rehabilitation. Here is a list of the team's players and the countries they represented.

Giant's Player	Country Represented
Moises Alou	Dominican Republic
Armando Benitez	Dominican Republic
Angel Chavez	Panama
Pedro Feliz	Dominican Republic
Omar Vizquel	Venezuela
Randy Winn	United States of America

April, 2006: Eddie Grant's Memorial Plaque is Recreated and Placed at AT&T Park

On Memorial Day 1921, a memorial plaque for Eddie Grant was unveiled at the Polo Grounds. The plaque was attached to a five-foot high monument stone in deep center field of the park. Grant played 10 Major League seasons, three with the New York Giants from 1913-15. When World War I broke out, Grant joined the Army. On the morning of October 5, 1918, just moments after he was given orders for a mission to relieve a fellow officer, an exploding shell ended his life. Grant was the only Major League player killed in the War. The plaque remained at the Polo Grounds until the Giants' last game on September 30, 1957. At 4:35 p.m., the final out was recorded. Fans poured onto the field and took any memento or souvenir that they could find, including prying Grant's Memorial Plaque from the monument. As far as can be determined, the plaque has never been found, despite myth, rumor and a lot of hard searching.

In March, 2006, Neil Hayes of the *Contra Costa Times* wrote about the "curse" of Eddie Grant. Some believe that the hex has haunted the Giants since they moved to San Francisco from the Polo Grounds, and is the reason they have not won the World Series. On at least two occasions, in 1994 and 2001, interested parties asked Giants' ownership to create an exact replica and place it somewhere at Candlestick Park, and later at AT&T Park. The Giants felt that the incident was related to New York Giants history and had no relevance in San Francisco. No action had been taken until Hayes' story appeared shortly before the 2006 season opened. In April 2006, the Giants must have taken the story to heart and a duplicate of Grant's memorial appeared on a wall outside the park without any fanfare or publicity. Giants' fans, of all generations, around the world, hope that Eddie can rest better and that the curse has been broken!

2006 Season: The Giants Feature Unique 40-40-40 Club

In baseball, the 40-40 Club connotes a very unique accomplishment with the membership being a very limited fraternity. In 2006, the Giants had a very unique combination that will forever be known as the 40-40-40 Club. The triple 40s referred to the ages of each of the starting outfielders in several games during the 2006 season. Left fielder Barry Bonds turned 42 in July 24, new center fielder Steve Finely turned 40 on March 1 and right fielder Moises Alou turned 40 on July 3. This was the oldest regular outfield in Major League Baseball history. It bested the record set by the Giants in 2005 by five years (Bonds, 41 / Grissom, 37 / Alou, 39).

2006: Bonds Hammers 714th and 715th Home Runs to Pass Babe Ruth

After hitting home run number 713, Barry Bonds had to sweat it out for a while before he could get back to a level of manageable normalcy. With the weight of the entire situation on his shoulders, and being surrounded by a media frenzy that would not quit, he went thirteen more days until he tied legendary slugger Babe Ruth for second place on the all-time list at 714. The blast did not come at home, but it occurred in the next best place, in the Bay Area at the Oakland Coliseum against the A's. Barry Bonds turned on a 1-1 pitch in the top of the second inning from Brad Halsey and put it over the right field wall on May 20.

Number 715 was eight days (May 28) later at AT&T Park against the Colorado Rockies. In his second at-bat of the day versus Byung-Hyun Kim, Bonds belted a drive to straight-away centerfield that bounced off a coupe, of fans and trickled down into the concession area. The shot was officially announced to be 445 feet in length. He rounded the bases to be met at home plate by his 16-year old son Nickoli. Because he was not hitting the home runs in droves like he once did, it looked as if Bonds would hit the monumental blast on the road, as the Giants were leaving for a week-long road trip right after the game; he did not disappoint the San Francisco fans. Bonds received two curtain calls from the devoted Giant's fans.

06/06/06: Schmidt Wins Award, Then Ties Franchise Game Strikeout Record

Jason Schmidt matched a 102 year-old Giants franchise (New York & San Francisco) record with 16 strikeouts in a game as he beat the Florida Marlins on 2-1. The high-point of the evening was when he fanned the final three batters of the game to escape a ninth-inning jam and preserve the Giant's win. Schmidt gave up consecutive singles to start the ninth, and a wild pitch put runners at second and third with none out. It looked certain that the Marlins may tie or even take the lead in the low-scoring contest; that just added to the drama. The ace then flexed his muscle and fanned Miguel Cabrera, Josh Willingham and Jeremy Hermida in succession to notch the victory. Schmidt tied the franchise record for strikeouts in a game set by Hall-of-Fame pitcher Christy Mathewson. On October 3, 1904, Mathewson set-down 16 St. Louis Cardinals. Schmidt also broke the San Francisco record of 15 strikeouts by Gaylord Perry on July 22, 1966, against the Philadelphia Phillies. One day earlier, the National League announced that Schmidt was the Pitcher of the Month Award winner for May. During the month, Schmidt was a perfect 4-0 with a 1.17 earned-run average.

06/25/06: Giants Pay Tribute to Four Milestones

The San Francisco Giants paid tribute to four of their 2006 team members in a pre-game ceremony on Sunday, June 25, prior to the games against the Oakland Athletics. Barry Bonds, Jason Schmidt, Moises Alou and Steve Finley all achieved personal milestones during the first half of the season. The milestones honored were:

♦ Barry Bonds

On May 28, he majestically clobbered the 715th home run of his career off of Colorado's Byung-Hyun Kim that allowed him to pass Babe Ruth for second place on the all-time home run list.

♦ Jason Schmidt

On June 6, he equaled a 102-year old Giant's franchise record when he struck out 16 Florida Marlins. That tied him with Hall-of-Famer Christy Mathewson who set the mark on October 3, 1904 vs. the St. Louis Cardinals. Schmidt's performance surpassed the San Francisco mark of 15, established by Gaylord Perry on July 22, 1966 vs. Philadelphia.

♦ Moises Alou

This season, Alou smashed his 300th career home run off of Houston's Brandon Backe in the first game of an April 13 doubleheader at AT&T Park.

♦ Steve Finley

On June 14 hit his 300th career home run off of Arizona's Claudio Vargas. With this shot, he became just the sixth member of Major League Baseball's 300/300 club, as he already had 316 career stolen bases at the time. He became the fifth member of the club who has played for the Giants, joining Willie Mays, Bobby Bonds, Barry Bonds and Reggie Sanders. Andre Dawson is the only 300/300 player.

Portwalk Plaques

On April 29, 2006, the Giants honored one of their greats when former closer Robb Nen's 300th career save was permanently enshrined on the portwalk behind the right field wall at AT&T Park. Nen's milestone was the 10th event in recent Giant's franchise history to be commemorated since the ballpark opened in 2000. Nen, who retired following the 2004 campaign, became the 16th Major League pitcher to register his 300th career save on August 6th, 2002 versus the Chicago Cubs. At the age of 32, he was the youngest pitcher to reach that milestone. Nen joined former teammate Barry Bonds as the only two players to have their feats acknowledged on the portwalk. Shortly after that on June 25th, the club acknowledged one more of Bond's feats and one by Jason Schmidt. Bonds, Nen and Schmidt are the only three to have individual plaques now. The latter two were not installed until September. Bonds' milestones account for six of the 12 moments in the AT&T Park era that are permanently displayed on the portwalk behind the right field arcade. A complete list of the 12 plaques, in the order they were installed, from the right field corner towards center field, is listed below.

Ballpark Opening Day, April 11, 2000

The then-named Pacific Bell Park opened. It was the first privately financed Major League ballpark to be built in 38 years.

2000 National League West Division Champions

The Giants won the division with a 97-65 record (.599), the best in Major League Baseball.

Barry Bonds' 500th Career Home Run

Bonds joined the "500 Home Run Club" with a two-run shot in the eighth inning off of Los Angeles' Terry Adams on April 17, 2001. The blast was also a game winner.

Barry Bonds: All-Time Single-Season Home Run Record

Bonds set the Major League single-season record for home runs with 73 in 2001.

Barry Bonds' 600th Career Home Run

Bonds became just the fourth player to reach the elite home run level when he connected off of Pittsburgh's Kip Wells on August 9, 2002.

2002 National League Champions

The Giants won their 18th National League pennant and made their 17th World Series appearance.

2003 National League Western Division Champions

The Giants became only the second team in franchise history, and ninth in Major League history, to go wire-to-wire and win the division. The club finished at 100-61 (.621).

Barry Bonds Ties Willie Mays Career Home Run Mark

Bonds hit his 660th career home run to tie his godfather, and former Giants great, Willie Mays for third place on the all-time home run list. The shot was off of Milwaukee's Matt Kinney on April 12, 2004.

Barry Bonds' 700th Career Home Run

Bonds ascended to the 700 home run plateau, becoming just the third member, with his solo clout off of San Diego's Jake Peavy on September 17, 2004.

Robb Nen's 300th Career Save

Nen became the youngest pitcher to reach 300 career saves on August 6, 2002 against the Chicago Cubs at Pacific Bell Park.

Barry Bonds' 715th Career Home Run

Bonds moved past Babe Ruth into sole possession of second place on the all-time home run list with number 715 on May 28, 2006 against Byung-Hyun Kim of the Colorado Rockies at AT&T Park.

Jason Schmidt's 16-Strikeout Game

Schmidt tied the all-time Giant's franchise record with 16 strikeouts in a game and broke the old San Francisco mark of 15 against the Florida Marlins on June 6, 2006 at AT&T Park.

Kirk Rueter: A Salute to "Woody"

On August 19, 2006, the Giants honored one of their all-time fan favorites, Kirk Rueter, for his 10 1/2 years of service with "Kirk Rueter Day." The left-handed hurler had a lifetime record o130 wins and 92 losses for a winning percentage of .586. But the story goes far beyond, just the win and loss record. "Woody" solidified himself in some unique places in the historical statistics of the game. Consider these figures that he achieved at the time of his release by the Giants on August 13, 2005:

- ◆ Rueter's .651 road winning percentage (69-37) was the fifth best among active pitchers in 2005. Only Pedro Martinez .715 (93-37), Roger Clemens .662 (157-80), Freddy Garcia .662 (45-23) and Tim Hudson .658 (48-25) had higher percentages.
- ◆ Rueter's overall career percentage of .586 (130-92) was the fifth best of any active left-hander in 2005. The other top four: Randy Johnson .656 (250-131), Andy Pettitte .643 (157-87), David Wells .605 (214-140) and Tom Glavine .602 (265- 175).
- ◆ Rueter's winning percentage was the best of any pitcher (since 1961) with at least 100 wins and fewer than four strikeouts (3.87) per nine innings pitched.

♦ Rueter's 130 victories were the third most of any pitcher (since 1961) with fewer than 1,000 career strikeouts (802). Only Scott McGregor (138 wins, 904 strikeouts) and Mike Caldwell (137 wins, 939 strikeouts) had more.

♦ Rueter averaged approximately 5 2/3 innings per start in his career. He is the only Major League Player ever to have at least 300 starts (327) and fewer than 10 complete games (four).

♦ Rueter is one of only two players in Major League Baseball history with at least 100 wins and fewer than five complete games. The only other is Oakland A's Hall-of-Fame reliever Rollie Fingers. He retired with 114 wins and four complete games. Fingers, known primarily a one of the best "firemen" or relievers during his career, saved 341 games. He started just 35 games early in his career between 1969 and 1971, with four completed.

In addition, back in 1993, when he was a rookie, Rueter won his first 10 consecutive starts for the Montreal Expos. This is good for second best all-time, bested by only Hooks Wiltse of the 1904 New York Giants (12-0).

Barry Bonds, Career

Just like the high level of play that his father demonstrated in the '60s and '70s, Barry Bonds kept the tradition going in the 1990s and into the new Century. Bonds possessed all of the tools that define a great player: power, speed, fielding ability, and throwing ability. A whole book could be written and certainly one whole chapter is this work could be dedicated to his exploits. Over the course of 20 years, he became baseball's most dangerous hitter and one of the best all-around players in the modern era of the game. As he strolls into the sunset of his career, he closes in on the all-time home run title -- although still in the shadow -- held by Hank Aaron. In the past few years injury, controversy and criticism have become barriers that have stood in his way.

His numbers say it all. In addition to the gaudy offensive statistics, there are eight Gold Glove awards, 13 All-Star Games and seven Most Valuable Player honors, four of them consecutive. During the 1996, season he became only the third member of the 40-40 club, having at least 40 home runs and 40 stolen bases in the same season. Bonds is also the only member of the career 500-500 club. In 2004 he walked an astounding 232 times, 120 of them intentional, making him the first player ever to surpass the 200-bases-on-balls mark in a single season. The feat catapulted him to first place on the all-time list.

When it came to home runs, Bonds broke the single season record of 70 in 2001, set by Mark McGwire in 1998, "going yard" an unfathomable 73 times. He is only the fourth player to join the "600 Club," the elite group of only four players in baseball history to hit over 600 home runs. On top of that, he is only the third player to enter the "700 Club," behind only Aaron (755) and having passed Babe Ruth (714).

After the 2004 season, he looked as if he was well within striking distance of Aaron's 755, sitting at 703. Needing only 53 to break the record didn't seem impossible to accomplish by the end of the 2005 or beginning of the 2006 season. However, at 2005 training camp, Bonds revealed that he required additional surgery on one of his knees. Two months later, he went under the knife again. It was his third surgery on the same knee since March of that year. His rigorous rehabilitation and optimistic outlook helped him return to the team in mid-September. He played in just 14 games, hitting five home runs. In late September, he decided to shut-down his season, as the Giants were eliminated from any playoff contention.

The 2006 season saw Bonds take the field as healthy as could be expected with his age and injury history. It was the final year of his contract with the Giants. Hints on his part, and speculation from the media and baseball experts indicate he was probably a better fit for the American League as a designated hitter, if he were to play in 2007. Both his age, coupled with the risk of everyday play on his surgically repaired knee, have led to this one theory about his future.

Here is a summary list the honors and accomplishments of Bonds (08/25/06):

♦ Has 725 career home runs

♦ Won an unprecedented seven National League Most Valuable Player awards ('90, '92, '93, 2001, '02, '03 and '04), with no other player winning more than three

♦ Third member of the exclusive 700 Home Run Club, joining Hall-of-Famers Hank Aaron and Babe Ruth

♦ Reached the hallowed 700 home run plateau on September 17, 2004, connecting for solo home run off San Diego's Jake Peavy

♦ By belting five home runs in just 42 at-bats in 2005, a ratio of one clout per 8.5 at-bats, advanced his lifetime mark to 12.91

♦ In 587 games from Opening Day, 2001 until the end of the 2005 season, hit .347 (585-for-1,684) with 494 runs, 214 home runs, 448 RBIs and 764 walks (287 intentional) while posting .556 on-base percentage and .805 slugging mark

♦ Tied his godfather, Willie Mays, for third on all-time home run list at 660 career clouts with a "Splash Hit" into McCovey Cove April 12, 2004 off of Milwaukee's Matt Kinney. Passed Mays the next day, again reaching the Cove with solo drive off Brewers' Ben Ford

♦ Hit a home run off of a record 429 different Major League pitchers, with Mark McGwire being a distant second at 362

♦ Owns Major League Baseball's single-season records for:
  • Home runs (73 in 2001)
  • Walks (232 in '04)
  • Intentional walks (120 in '04)
  • On-base percentage (.609 in '04)
  • Slugging percentage (.863 in '01)
  • Home run ratio (6.52 in '01)
  • Home run percentage (12.06 in '04)

- Established a Major League record with 13 consecutive seasons with at least 30 home runs, reaching the plateau every year from 1992-2004

- Belted at least 30 home runs in 14 seasons overall, one shy of Aaron's Major League standard of 15 different 30-home run campaigns

- Achieved 40 home runs in a season eight times, tying Aaron's National League record. Ruth holds Major League mark with 11 such years

- In 2004, when he hammered 45 home runs and struck out only 41 times, Bonds became just the fifth player ever (10th occurrence) to hit at least 40 roundtrippers and strike out less times than he hit a home run

- Hit 20 or more home runs in a season 17 times, three behind Aaron's Major League mark

- Posted a National League record 12 seasons with 100 or more RBIs

- In 2004, became just the third player in baseball history to post at least 100 RBIs (101) in season in which he had less than 400 at-bats (373)

- Holds National League mark with 13 seasons of 100 or more walks, tied with Babe Ruth for the Major League standard

- Established Major League career records with 2,411 walks and 644 intentional walks

- Had 68 multi-home run games to rank second in that category on the all-time list, behind only Ruth (72)

- Connected for 308 home runs after his 35th birthday (in 2000), most by any player after that age in Major League history

- One of just seven players in Major League history to reach base safely 5,000 times, reaching 5,418 times via a hit, walk or hit-by-pitch

- Only the fourth Giant to win a National League batting crown in franchise history. He was the first player in franchise history to capture more than one title ('02 and '04)

♦ With a .362 batting average in 2004, he became oldest player ever to lead a league in hitting at 40 years and 71 days old

♦ By posting an .800-plus slugging percentage in both 2001 and 2004, Bonds joined Babe Ruth ('20 and '21) as the only players ever to crest the .800 slugging mark twice

♦ Led the National League in both slugging and on-base percentage for four consecutive seasons between 2001-04. Bonds became just the third Major Leaguer to accomplish this feat

♦ Selected as a 13-time All-Star Game participant

♦ Won Rawlings Gold Glove eight times

♦ Garnered 12 Silver Slugger Awards

♦ Named "Player of the Decade" for the 1990s by *The Sporting News*

♦ Earned the "Players Choice Award" as player of the year in 2001 and 2004 and "National League Player of Year" five times ('92, '93, '01, '02 and '04)

♦ Sole member of 500 home run / 500 steal club

♦ Established himself as most prolific home run hitter in San Francisco club history with 532 clouts in a Giants uniform. Bonds has the second highest in franchise history, behind only the 646 hit by Mays with New York and San Francisco

♦ Became only the second member of 40-40 club and the only National Leaguer to accomplish feat after hitting 42 home runs and stealing 40 bases in 1996

♦ Has reached the 30-30 plateau five times in career ('90, '92, '95, '96 and '97), joining his late father Bobby ('69, '73, '75, '77 and '78) as the only five-time 30-30 men in Major League history

♦ Became just the fourth Giant to start at least 13 season openers with club by making Opening Day start in left field in 2006 at San Diego, joining Willie Mays (19 openers), Mel Ott (18) and Willie McCovey (15)

♦ Is only the 25th player in Major League history to amass 2,000 hits and 400 home runs in a career. Bonds is also one of just seven players to accumulate 2,000 hits, 200 home runs and 400 stolen bases

♦ Hit a home run in 36 Major League parks during career, with Seattle's Kingdome and San Juan, Puerto Rico's Hiram Bithorn Stadium being the only facilities in which he has played during regular season and not hit a home run

♦ Selected as a member of the All-1990s, All-2000s and All-Time 50th Anniversary San Francisco Giants teams. A sure Hall-of-Fame inductee

2007 All-Star Game Schedule for AT&T Park

Since AT&T Park (Pacific Bell / SBC Park) opened in 2000, it had always been rumored that the Giants would host an All-Star Game in the near future. Amidst these rumors, in February 2005, Commissioner Bud Selig made it official, the Giants would host the 2007 Major League Baseball All-Star Game on July 10, 2007. This marks the first time the Giants will have hosted the event since 1984 (Candlestick Park), and only the third in San Francisco history. The event coincides with the teams' golden anniversary celebration in San Francisco.

Boy, How This Game Has Changed: Marketing and Revenue

Just as society has changed over the past 50 years, baseball has moved right along, as well, growing at seemingly exponential rates. In the age of high-priced ballplayers, teams look for the maximization of their revenue streams. In addition, they look for the utmost exposure of their product, seeking new demographic groups to lure as fans.

To some fans who attend sporting events in person, the game itself is not enough of an attraction to get them to consistently bring themselves and / or their families to the park. Teams have recognized these preferences and strive to look for ways to make each patron's visit more comfortable, convenient and memorable. In short, they want the fan to come back again and again. Having a state-of-the-art facility is incumbent to survival for the sports fan dollar. The Giants built their own. Consequently, they also have a mortgage to pay.

Here is a list of changes that truly exhibit how different the game experience off the field is today, compared to say when you attended your first game in the 1960s, 1970s or even the 1980s. I guarantee it! Teams use a multitude of methods to entertain provide convenience.

The Virtual World

♦ Team Internet Website

Fans can find a wealth of information, history, statistics and news about the Giants and all of Major League Baseball here. Fans can order and print the actual admission tickets right on their own printer at home or in the office. In addition, fans can order merchandise in a secure environment with just a few clicks of the mouse.

♦ Fan Ticket Maximization Programs (Web Based)

Dubbed as the "Double Play" Ticket Window, fans wishing to buy, sell or trade game tickets can easily find other fans and conduct a transaction here. Additionally, fans can also find others to share their season tickets with via an online networking program called the "Ticket Partner Zone." The "Ticket Relay" program allows fans to electronically transfer tickets via e-mail right up until game time.

♦ Message Boards / Web logs (Web Based)

Fans can express their opinions about players, management, the team and other pertinent topics on the team's official site. In addition, some fans start their own websites that allow "blogging" and sharing of information and ideas.

- Game Broadcasts and Game Logs (Web Based)

  Fans no longer need a radio to listen to the game anymore. The Internet broadcasts Giants' games anywhere there is a computer. In addition, the advent of satellite radio also allows for personal programming preferences worldwide with any of two major providers. Many sites offer "game logs" or glogs that track the game [pitch-by-pitch with more information, statistics and detail that even the most fervent of stat heads could digest.

At the Game / Ballpark

- Ballpark Tours

  Daily tours of the park are offered, depending on the team's schedule and area availability. Fans are shown all of the key features and amenities that make up the facility, including: dugouts, luxury boxes, restaurants and views front just about every seat angle.

- Fan / Kid Lot

  Located on the Promenade Level, above the left field bleachers, the fan lot is an interactive play area for children and adults. Fans of all ages can enjoy a slide into home plate from one of the four slides inside the 80-foot wooden soda bottle; stroll up to the world's largest baseball glove, a vintage three-finger classic, get an autograph rubbing from some of their favorite all-time Giants or Build-A-Bear (or Seal); there is also the speed-pitch booth and fan photo booth. Kids can run the bases inside "Little Giants Park." The Fan Lot offers guests not only a great view of the game, but also views of the San Francisco skyline, Bay Bridge and San Francisco Bay.

- Luxury Suites / Club Level

  Located just above the AAA Club Level, the park's 67 private luxury suites provide the ultimate environment to entertain friends, family or business associates. Suites vary in size, holding from 12 to 21 people and are equipped with televisions, radios, CD players, dual-line telephones, wet bars and refrigerators. Other amenities include: in-suite catering, AAA Club Level access, concierge service and priority reserved parking spaces.

♦ Cove Party Boat Tours

Fans no longer have to go to the game in order to go to the game. Several party boat tour companies provide the means for a leisurely cruise on the Bay, including an extended anchor in the McCovey Cove while the game is in progress.

♦ Slumber Party

Fans can sleep for one night on the plush green grass of their favorite baseball park, watch movies on the scoreboard and wake to a catered breakfast cooked by Giants' Hall-of-Famer Orlando Cepeda and Tito Fuentes.

♦ "Dog Days"

Canine fans get a pass to enjoy the action for one game each August. This tradition originally started back at Candlestick Park, is dubbed "The Dog Days of Summer."

♦ Meeting / Conference: Business Center

Located on the Suite Level, the Business Center provides a range of services for suiteholders, Field Club and AAA Club members including faxing, copying and modem connections. Concierge services are also available.

♦ Upscale Food / Beer

In today's game, hot dogs, peanuts and cotton candy are not the norm. Fans can enjoy just about any type of food imaginable while watching a game. Designer label beers of all types are also available. AT&T Park serves 24 different types of hot dogs.

♦ Health Center

The Health Center is located on the Portwalk near the Lefty O'Doul Bridge. In addition to offering medical evaluations, this facility provides a full range of occupational health, physical therapy and radiology services. The Center also supports the first aid services at the park.

♦ Corporate Sponsorship / Advertisement

Advertising and sponsorship have become a major part of the game, and represent an enormous source of revenue for the club. Signage can be seen from the moment a fan gets within blocks of the park until they are seated to watch the game. No stone (wall) is left unturned for the opportunity to let you know who brought you this half inning, promotion, interview, lineup or the game.

The Off Season

♦ Winter / Summer Fanfests

In addition to the ability to purchase upcoming season game tickets, the Giants Winter Fanfest features appearances by Giants' players, alumni, management and broadcasters throughout the day to sign autographs, take photos and participate in live interviews. Other activities include Giants merchandise sales, silent auctions of baseball memorabilia, batting and pitching cages and interactive games. The Giants also hold an in season mid-summer Fanfest each year.

♦ Spring Training Tour Packages

Spring training trips to sunny Arizona have become the favored vacation destination for many fans and families. The sport has seen exponential growth in the past 20 years. No longer are players isolated in a God forbidden desert location. Fans can experience all of the luxuries associated with other upscale vacation spots and regular season baseball games. Hotels, restaurants and the ballparks themselves lend a feeling of style, elegance and charm. These trips are attractive because of the short distance from the San Francisco Bay Area, allowing fans to make a long weekend out of it.

♦ Ballpark Party Rental

The ballpark, and all of its amenities can be rented for a corporate event or private party. The ballpark can accommodate parties from as intimate as ten to more than 40,000. The park, with many of its various attraction venues and levels, can be rented on non-game days for conferences, meetings, trade shows, private parties and weddings. Events can be held almost anywhere in the ballpark from the field to the Fan Lot to the Club Level and even inside the clubhouses. The Dioceses of San Francisco held a Roman Catholic mass for over 40,000 in 2003.

Other

♦ Retail Store Outlets

The Giants have a large retail store located adjacent to the ballpark, which is their flagship. In addition, they have several other stores located in malls and shopping areas throughout northern California for their fans to shop for the latest clothing and souvenirs.

♦ Kids Baseball Clinics

The Giants bring their show on the road to communities from Fresno to Shasta with key alumni and players providing baseball instruction to children.

♦ Top Attraction Concerts

The Giants have such a wonderful venue in SBC Park. They try to utilize it for events other than baseball when not in use or during the off-season. Fans enjoy the luxury that the park offers for a wide variety of events. Some of the top entertainment acts in the music world have appeared at Pacific Bell / SBC / AT&T Park. In 2002, the Rolling Stones celebrated their 40th Anniversary Tour with a two-night gig in November. They returned again in the fall of 2005. In the summer of 2003, "The Boss" himself, Bruce Springsteen played to a packed house. Other performers included Green Day and Dave Matthews.

Giants' Memorabilia is Quite Popular

Talking about any team would not be complete without the mention of team and player collectibles. Fans have collected team items since the beginning of competitive sports. Collectors are passionate and quite resourceful when it comes to locating items they need for their collections.

Over the years baseball cards have been popular. In the older days, there was one company, Topps, and one release each year. Over the past 25 years, the market has seen an exponential proliferation of companies and a seemingly limitless number of releases from each. Cards of the Giants' Hall-of-Famers continue to be popular with an adult crowd who remember their heroes while they were youngsters.

Some older items that remain popular and elusive are the felt pennants from the 1950s and 1960s. The original bobble head dolls command a premium, as well, especially the Willie Mays variation. The new bobble heads, many distributed at Giants' games, are fan favorites. They are, however, produced in larger quantities and do not have the rarity and value of the originals.

One unique subgroup is the hat pin collectors. These small items that are approximately the size of a quarter or half-dollar remain one of the most popular collectibles. They have transcended generations. There is an almost endless supply of different types. Every team and player milestone is celebrated by pins. Some are produced by the team for give aways or sale. Some are produced by licensed vendors. Still more are produced without authorization and distributed. Pins honoring all of Barry Bonds' accomplishments flooded the market with a steady stream.

Some other popular collectibles are: All-Star Game tickets, World Series tickets, playoff tickets and home run balls. Other tickets to notable performances such as no-hitters, 3,000 hit games or any of a number of Barry Bonds' significant home run games are sought. Full tickets are more valuable than stubs. The significant home runs for Bonds include home runs No. 71 and No. 73 from the 2001 season, and career home runs Nos. 500, 600, 660, 661, 700, 714 and 715.

Reality Television Shows

Early in the new century, reality television shows became a phenomena and the norm for all broadcast stations. Viewing audiences for some of these shows drew record numbers. Many shows were participatory for "everyday people," but several also followed celebrities and stars with a camera everywhere they went in their lives. For Barry Bonds, the latter applied. In April 2006, ESPN Entertainment chronicled his daily life, relationships, workouts, interactions with teammates and fans, among the many facets of his life, entitled "Bonds on Bonds." It ran on ESPN2.

Giant's Honor Past Teams with Reunions

The Giants have always honored their history and the outstanding players who have captured the headlines. In addition to honoring the individuals, they have also recognized special teams that have achieved success during the franchise's history. Here are the honorees that had ceremonies at Pacific Bell / SBC / AT&T Park:

♦ Remember '51: 1951 National League Champions (2002)

This was the team that staged a great late season rally to catch the Brooklyn Dodgers. They defeated the Dodgers in perhaps the most memorable ending in baseball history as Bobby Thomson hit the "shot heard 'round the world." It was celebrated in 2002 as it was postponed from 2001 due to the 9/11 tragedy. A large plaque honoring the team hangs in the upper reaches of left field at AT&T Park.

♦ 1954 World Champions (2004)

This is the Giants' last World Championship team. The heavy underdogs swept the mighty Cleveland Indians in the World Series 4-0. Willie Mays made perhaps the greatest catch in baseball history in the eighth inning of Game 1 off the bat of Vic Wertz, 473 feet from home plate in the deepest cavern of the Polo Grounds in straight away center field.

♦ 1962 National League Champions (2002)

This is perhaps the best all-around Giants' team to ever take the field in San Francisco. Young manager Alvin Dark, a member of many other great Giants' teams as a player, led the club to a 103 win season. It all ended with heartbreak in the glove of the Yankees' Bobby Richardson.

♦ 1978 Western Division Contenders (2003)

This club fell just short of winning the National League's Western Division. However, they revitalized the franchise that had been through some lean times and were in the race all throughout the summer.

San Francisco Giants' Nicknames

No sport has a richer history of nicknames than baseball. From all-time greats to obscure players, nicknames have, and still are, part of the legend and lore of baseball. They can describe a personality of a player.

It may describe a certain place he is from. It can even be a play on his real name. Whatever the case, it is as much a part of the game as the seventh-inning stretch or the national anthem.

Over the years, the San Francisco Giants have had many colorful players wear their uniform. With this, they have had some pretty unique nicknames to go along with the characters they referred to. Here are some of them:

Andrews, Rob, "Rock"
Baker, Dusty, "Hard Bake," "Johnnie B."
Beck, Rod, "Shooter"
Bedrosian, Steve, "Bedrock"
Berenguer, Juan, "Senor Smoke"
Blue, Vida, "True"
Brenly, Bob, "BB"
Brown, Ollie, "Downtown"
Carlton, Steve, "Lefty"
Carter, Gary, "The Kid"
Cepeda, Orlando, "Baby Bull," "Cha-Cha"
Clark, Jack, "Ripper"
Clark, Will, "The Thrill," "The Natural"
Evans, Darrell, "Howdy"
Felder, Mike, "Tiny"
Galarraga, Andres, "Big Cat"
Gallagher, Alan, "Dirty Al"
Gossage, Rich, "Goose"
Halicki, Ed, "Ho-Ho"
Heaverlo, Dave, "Tuna"
Hershiser, Orel, "Bulldog"
Johnson, Erik, "EJ"
Jones, Sam, "Sad," "Toothpick"
Kuiper, Duane, "Smooth"
LaCoss, Mike, "Buffy"
Laskey, Bill, "Tree"

LeMaster, Johnnie, "Johnnie Lee"
Leonard, Jeffrey, "Hac-Man"
Lewis, Darren, "D Lew"
Madlock, Bill, "Mad Dog"
Marichal, Juan, "Dominican Dandy"
Matthews, Gary, "Sarge"
Mays, Willie, "Say Hey Kid," "Buck," "Chico"
McCovey, Willie, "Stretch," "Big Mac"
McDowell, Sam, "Sudden"
Minton, Greg, "Moon Man"
Montefusco, John, "The Count"
Nicosia, Steve, "Nick"
Nokes, Matt, "Noker"
Reuschel, Rick, "Big Daddy"
Righetti, Dave, "Rags"
Robinson, Don, "Caveman"
Rodriguez, Felix, "FRod"
Sadek, Mike, "The Sheik"
Sanders, Deion, "Prime Time," "Neon Deion"
Shinjo, Tsuyoshi, "Elvis"
Wagner, Leon, "Daddy Wags"

Chapter 12: San Francisco Giants' Tributes to the Great Willies

Willie Mays Plaza / Gate

In August 1998, the Giants unveiled a design for a spectacular Willie Mays sculpture at Pacific Bell Park and announce a change in ballpark's official address from "One Willie Mays Plaza" to "24 Willie Mays Plaza" in honor of the number Mays wore during his playing career. As everyone knows, the team strongly embraces their history and heritage. The Giants do a great job of remembering their past. The entrance of the park is located at 24 Willie Mays Plaza to recognize the best player in team history.

The statue is part of the magnificent Willie Mays Plaza, located at the corner of Third and King streets. The plaza also features 24 palm trees in recognition of Mays' jersey number and is home to a nine-foot bronze sculpture of the famous ballplayer. The statue was commissioned by Peter and Debby Magowan and created by William Behrends, a well-known American sculptor and longtime Mays admirer.

The statue was dedicated on the day that the park officially opened, March 31, 2000. The Giants played an exhibition game that night against the Milwaukee Brewers. The next day, April 1, the Giants hosted the mighty New York Yankees in their first San Francisco appearance since Game 7 of the 1962 World Series.

McCovey Point at China Basin Park

They called him "Stretch" or "Big Mac" and never were nicknames more of a descriptor for a player. Willie McCovey didn't just stretch above the players of his time, he towered over them. This gentle man always looked down upon the world with a smile of genuine humility over his lofty baseball deeds. With his awesome swing, McCovey walloped many memorable home runs, 521 in all. His inspirational play in a career that stretched through parts of four decades resulted in the establishment of the annual Willie Mac Award by San Francisco. The award, chosen by a vote of fellow teammates, is the highest honor a Giants' player can receive.

On the other side of the cove from SBC Park, beyond the Lefty O'Doul Plaza entrance, fans can walk over the Lefty O'Doul Bridge that takes them to China Basin Park at McCovey Point. O'Doul, a San Francisco native, is a potential American Baseball Hall-of-Famer, member of the Japanese Baseball Hall-of-Fame and major contributor to the game. He started out his career as a successful pitcher until he hurt his arm and was forced to become a full-time outfielder and proceeded to become one of the most feared hitters of his time.

At McCovey Point, the Giants have honored Willie with a bronze statue as well as a 1,500-foot long circular wall that has markers in the shape of home plate to commemorate each season the Giants spent in San Francisco prior to Pacific Bell Park (1958-1999) at Seals Stadium and Candlestick Park. Each marker lists the opening day lineup, each rostered player for the season, manager and coaches, statistical leaders, and significant achievements during the year. The larger-than-life image of this living legend has been carved in bronze and placed as the centerpiece of McCovey Point at China Basin Park, keeping watch over McCovey Cove. China Basin Park is a popular pre and post-game gathering spot for Giants fans young and old. Families can picnic along the shores of the cove, play a game of catch on the green or stroll along the Giants History Walk while enjoying breathtaking views of

AT&T Park and San Francisco Bay. Visible from inside the ballpark, the McCovey statue is lit at night, shining like a beacon into the present from the Giants' treasured seasons of the past.

McCovey Cove "Splash Landings" - Giants' Players

Located just over the 24 foot (in honor of Willie Mays' number 24) wall that is a scant 309 feet from home plate, over the Promenade seats, beyond the Portwalk, "McCovey Cove" nestles the most beautiful baseball park in the world. This small body of water, connected to San Francisco Bay, is popular with sea-faring fans.

Over the years, several Giants' players have been able to drive the ball into the cove. When the ballpark design was first announced, it seemed as if batters could just reach out and touch the water. Everyone thought that a splashing would be an almost daily occurrence. Time has proven that it really does take a good poke to get the ball out to the water. This is primarily due to the height needed to get the ball over the wall and into the water, on a fly.

The feat even has its own scoreboard in the far right field corner, keeping a cumulative tab. Here is a complete list of "Splash Landings."

#	Giant's Hitter	Date	Opponent	Pitcher
41	Barry Bonds	08/21/06	Arizona	Livan Hernandez
40	Barry Bonds	09/18/05	Los Angeles	Hong-Chih Kuo
39	Randy Winn	09/14/05	San Diego	Woody Williams
38	Michael Tucker	04/09/05	Colorado	Scott Dohmann
37	Barry Bonds	08/03/04	Cincinnati	Cory Lidle
36	Barry Bonds	07/30/04	St. Louis	Chris Carpenter
35	A.J. Pierzynski	07/06/04	Colorado	Denny Stark
34	Michael Tucker	05/30/04	Colorado	Joe Kennedy
33	Barry Bonds	04/13/04	Milwaukee	Ben Ford

32	Barry Bonds	04/12/04	Milwaukee	Matt Kinney
31	Barry Bonds	09/13/03	Milwaukee	Doug Davis
30	Barry Bonds	08/19/03	Atlanta	Ray King
29	Barry Bonds	08/08/03	Philadelphia	Jose Mesa
28	Jose Cruz, Jr.	07/08/03	St. Louis	Dan Haren
27	Barry Bonds	06/27/03	Oakland	Ted Lilly
26	J.T. Snow	06/05/03	Minnesota	Kyle Lohse
25	Barry Bonds	04/24/03	Chicago (N)	Matt Clement
24	Barry Bonds	04/14/03	Houston	Wade Miller
23	Barry Bonds	10/12/02	St. Louis	Chuck Finley
22	Barry Bonds	09/28/02	Houston	Jeriome Robertson
21	Barry Bonds	09/08/02	Arizona	Brian Anderson
20	Barry Bonds	05/18/02	Florida	Vic Darensbourg
19	Barry Bonds	05/18/02	Florida	Brad Penny
18	Barry Bonds	05/13/02	Atlanta	Kevin Millwood
17	Barry Bonds	09/29/01	San Diego	Chuck McElroy
16	Barry Bonds	08/31/01	Colorado	John Thomson
15	Barry Bonds	08/14/01	Florida	Ricky Bones
14	Barry Bonds	08/04/01	Philadelphia	Nelson Figueroa
13	Felipe Crespo	07/08/01	Milwaukee	Curtis Leskanic
12	Barry Bonds	06/12/01	Anaheim	Pat Rapp
11	Barry Bonds	05/30/01	Arizona	Robert Ellis
10	Felipe Crespo	05/28/01	Arizona	Bret Prinz
9	Barry Bonds	05/24/01	Colorado	John Thomson
8	Barry Bonds	04/18/01	Los Angeles	Chan Ho Park
7	Barry Bonds	04/17/01	Los Angeles	Terry Adams
6	Barry Bonds	09/20/00	Cincinnati	Steve Parris
5	Barry Bonds	07/19/00	San Diego	Brian Meadows
4	Barry Bonds	05/24/00	Montreal	Mike Thurman
3	Barry Bonds	05/10/00	St. Louis	Heathcliff Slocumb
2	Barry Bonds	05/10/00	St. Louis	Andy Benes
1	Barry Bonds	05/01/00	New York (N)	Rich Rodriguez
Ex	Barry Bonds	04/01/00	New York (A)	Andy Pettitte

McCovey Cove "Splash Landings"
- San Francisco Opponents

Opponent home runs into McCovey Cove
Not counted as official Splash Hits

#	Hitter	Date	Opponent	Giant's Pitcher
12	Carlos Delgado	07/23/05	Florida	Brad Hennessey
11	Larry Walker	07/08/05	St. Louis	Jason Schmidt
10	Russell Branyan	04/23/05	Milwaukee	Brett Tomko
9	Alex Cora	09/25/04	Los Angeles	Brad Hennessey
8	Cliff Floyd	08/21/04	New York (N)	Brett Tomko
7	Corey Patterson	08/07/04	Chicago (N)	Tyler Walker
6	Hee Seop Choi	04/30/04	Florida	Kevin Correia
5	Ryan Klesko	04/09/03	San Diego	Ryan Jensen
4	Luis Gonzalez	05/30/02	Arizona	Kirk Rueter
3	Mark Grace	05/28/01	Arizona	Tim Worrell
2	Luis Gonzalez	09/23/00	Arizona	Shawn Estes
1	Todd Hundley	06/30/00	Los Angeles	Robb Nen
Ex	Jorge Posada	04/01/00	New York (A)	Joe Nathan

Chapter 13: Brief Overview of San Francisco Giant's Home Parks

Seals Stadium (1958 - 59)

In 1930, Seals Stadium was constructed in the Mission District of San Francisco. The stadium was built for the Pacific Coast League's (AAA) San Francisco Seals. The park was built with a combination of steel and concrete, and had a capacity of 18,600 when it opened on April 7, 1931. At that time, the city actually had two PCL teams, with the San Francisco Missions (a.k.a. Missions Reds) also playing at the park as a home team. The Seals became the sole tenant in 1938 when the Reds moved to Hollywood and became the Stars.

The park had a simple single-deck design coupled with elegant architectural stonework on the exterior. It provided fans with an impressive view of the neighborhood. The grandstand extended down both the base lines, and there was a small bleacher section located in right field. Seals Stadium also had lights. The park did not have a roof because daily temperatures were always comfortable, and there was little rainfall. This section of the City was said to have the best overall weather.

The scoreboard was located in centerfield above the hitter's backdrop. The stadium had three clubhouses, but only one was occupied after the Missions moved out. With long distances down the foul lines and an average distance to center, as well as a roofless, wide open grandstand, Seals Stadium was an extreme contrast to the Giants' previous home in Coogan's Bluff, the Polo Grounds. The outfield fences were angled inward, perpendicular to their respective portions of the grandstand, so that the power alleys were relatively modest in length; old Wrigley Field in Los Angeles (PCL) was laid out in almost the same exact fashion. There was a sharp angle in the fence in front of the center field scoreboard. The building in the right field corner of Seals Stadium contained the teams' offices. In back of the stadium there was a tall Hamm's Beer brewery, of "From the land of sky blue waters" fame. The left field bleachers were added when the Giants arrived, but the seating capacity of 22,900 was still inadequate for Major League expectations.

The Seals continued to play in the park until the New York Giants relocated to San Francisco from New York. Their last minor league game at the park was on September 13, 1957. The first Giants' game was on April 15, 1958. The Giants played at Seals Stadium for two years, attracting over two million fans before moving to their new home Candlestick Park in 1960. The Giants last game at Seals Stadium was on September 20, 1959. The ballpark was demolished in November, 1959, only a few months after the Giants moved out. It is now the site of commercial stores. The fold-down reserve seating and the light stanchions from the park are still being used today at Cheney Stadium in Tacoma, Washington.

Candlestick Park (1960 - 99)

Candlestick Park had its origins in the shady dealings that induced the New York Giants to move to the West Coast in 1958. A cunning developer named Charles Harney got the mayor of San Francisco to offer the Giants a large plot of rocky and muddy land on the San

Francisco Bay for a new stadium with plenty of parking space. He failed to inform the mayor or Giants' officials of the notorious fierce winds and bone-chilling night temperatures (even in summer) that plagued that area.

The new stadium took two years to complete, and during the interim, the Giants played in Seals Stadium. Candlestick Park in many ways was the standard of a modern baseball stadium, with a symmetrical structure and field layout, an acute-angle grandstand configuration, a small "roofette," and constructed primarily with concrete. Although modern, it was the very last Major League stadium built with supporting columns. Almost half of the lower deck was "in the shade," and a number of seats had what would be characterized as obstructed views. In terms of design, Candlestick Park stood out in two ways: 1.) The curvature of the grandstand arc behind home plate was extremely broad, almost as big as the Giants' old home in the Polo Grounds and 2.) The first deck extended way out beyond the left field fence and made a broad arc toward center field. This design resembled a football oval and was probably intended to lure the San Francisco 49ers to play there, but this did not happen until 11 years after the stadium opened. The stadium design was certainly ill-suited to baseball fans, who had to sit far away from the action. The acres of foul ground also impacted players' batting averages, with many balls being caught that would have extended far into the stands if a normal layout existed.

Early on, Candlestick Park became the object of ridicule and scorn after the horrendous winds blew Giants' pitcher Stu Miller off the mound during the 1961 All-Star Game. Although the original field dimensions were quite deep (420 feet to center field and 397 feet to the power alleys), the outfield fence was moved inward one year after the stadium opened, especially in the power alleys. Even with the shorter fences, the wind made this ballpark very unfavorable to batters, and probably reduced the lifetime home run record of Giants' slugger Willie Mays by at least a hundred. This is a conservative estimate. At 660, Mays fell short of both Babe Ruth's 714 and Hank Aaron's 755 totals. Because of the chilly, windy evenings at Candlestick, the Giants played most of their games during the day, even as most other teams shifted to mostly night schedules during the 1970s and 1980s.

In 1971 Candlestick Park was under construction additions to make room for the San Francisco 49ers, who finally decided to leave Kezar Stadium. The second deck was extended all the way around the outfield, with the front edge hanging right in back of the right field fence. Underneath it on the right field side was a large retractable grandstand section that, when pushed forward for football games, met flush with the upper deck to create one enormous deck on the north side of the field (This innovative retractable seating system was later adopted at the Metrodome and Pro Player Stadium, and was also imitated on a smaller scale at several other stadiums.). A new press box was built at the top of the second deck along the left side. As a result of the expansion, Candlestick Park assumed a sort of rounded triangular shape, somewhat resembling Yankee Stadium. Even though it was fully enclosed after 1971, the stadium remained plagued by unpredictable high winds swirling throughout. Artificial turf was also installed at that time, but the Giants and the 49ers quite sensibly reversed their decision in 1979 and put real grass back in. Consequently, Candlestick Park became one of the first stadiums to join the "back to nature" movement.

For many years the Giants languished in obscurity, but in 1989 the team experienced a resurgence and made it to the World Series again, this time against their cross-Bay rivals, the Oakland Athletics. The "Bay Bridge Series" was rudely interrupted by a massive earthquake. When it was over, several large chunks of concrete fell down, but somehow managed to miss any of the spectators. This disaster forced postponement of the World Series for almost two weeks. Game 3 is still the only World Series Game to ever be postponed due to a natural disaster.

In 1993, when new owner Peter Magowan took over, he strived to make the park a more appealing venue (if that was possible). Temporary bleachers were installed in back of the left field fence and fans were able to sit a little closer to the action. That was the same year the Giants signed superstar slugger Barry Bonds, but it wasn't until 1997 that they managed to win another divisional title. Being close to Silicon Valley, it was probably inevitable that San Francisco would succumb to the great high-tech corporate name sell-out of the 1990s. The computer networking company 3Com won the bidding and got their name tacked on in 1995. During the 1990s, the Giants put together a creative deal that led to the construction of their beautiful new home at Pacific Bell Park, on the south side of downtown San Francisco. They said goodbye and good riddance to Candlestick Park at the end of the 1999 season.

AT&T Park <f.k.a. Pacific Bell Park / SBC Park>

"Shangri-La." AT&T Park is widely regarded as the finest of all the retro, neoclassical baseball parks built in the last decade. It is beautiful in every way, from the scenic backdrop of San Francisco Bay to the palm trees that line the front plaza to the outer brick façade construction. The huge old-style fielder's mitt behind the left field bleachers is a marvelous touch, along with a kids' playground behind the bleachers. This attraction is complete with a mini baseball stadium, baseball diamond and video screen. This is a welcome stop for parents who look to keep restless kids occupied when the action on the field lags or the cotton candy runs out.

SBC Park is built in what was the old "China Basin" area of San Francisco. In the City's early years, the area where the park now stands was part of the San Francisco Bay. Sand from Rincon Hill (which anchors the western end of the Bay Bridge) and rubble from the 1906 earthquake are believed to have been used as landfill to create the parcel in the late 19th century. The area was then used primarily for shipping and industrial purposes. The Pacific Mail Steamship Company imported silk, tea, rice and opium from Asia to the United States to a dock at the foot of Brannan Street. The dominance of Asian commerce around the Brannan Street wharf led to the area being called China

Basin. Just west of the ballpark site, the Southern Pacific Railroad built its headquarters (1867) next to the rail yards at Fourth and Townsend streets. In 1915, Southern Pacific opened a mission-style passenger terminal at Third and Townsend streets.

Just as Yankee Stadium became known as "The House That Ruth Built," SBC Park may someday become known as "The House That Bonds Built." Both players are/were pull-hitting left-handed sluggers, but the very short 309-foot distance to right field in AT&T Park is offset by the 24-foot height of the wall plus the prevailing winds that, at times, blow from right to left field. The distance to the left field fence is slightly longer than average, but the 382-foot marker exaggerates that a little, since it is positioned much closer to center field than to the left field corner. The very deep (421-foot) distance to the corner on the right side of center field is a welcome (and rare, these days) opportunity for triples and inside-the-park home runs. Some say that AT&T Park is decidedly unfriendly to batters as exemplified by the low home run totals over its first few seasons.

The combination of the asymmetrical outfield dimensions plus the proximity to the bay waters makes this an utterly unique ballpark. Where else do baseball spectators get around in kayaks? The seats are very close to the playing field, and the distance behind home plate is only 54 feet; there is a brick wall behind the below-ground-level ultra-close box seats, however, suggesting that there may be a plan to remove these seats and create more room in back of home plate later on. The only noticeable downside may be putting the bullpens along the foul lines exposes relief pitchers to line drives, especially in a park where foul territory is so scant.

One feature that makes AT&T Park particularly attractive is that it was built almost entirely with private financing. The total construction cost was reported to be $319 million, and the San Francisco municipal government kicked in a mere $15 million as a loan guarantee. With an ambitious financing plan in place, Peter Magowan joined club

Executive Vice President and Chief Operating Officer Larry Baer in orchestrating a marketing campaign that reaped 29,500 season ticket holders, including 15,000 Charter Seat members. To put those figures in perspective, only three previous times in franchise history had the Giants sold more than even 10,000 season tickets, with an all-time high of 13,200 in 1994. What's more, the Charter Seat total more than tripled the previous record for a Major League Baseball team.

From the perspective of baseball franchise owners, however, this is a major embarrassment, and some have suggested that Bud Selig will delayed holding an All-Star Game in San Francisco for as long as possible. In its first two years in operation, Pacific Bell Park was sold out for almost every single game and the attendance figures for every game was exactly the same: 40,930. Since then, the capacity has been increased by several hundred, without any newly built permanent seats. Increase in attendance is attributed to the allowance of more standing-room-only spectators throughout. Average attendance relative to capacity is always in excess of 95 percent and usually close to 98 percent, posting even higher attendance percentage figures than Fenway Park in Boston. Official attendance at almost every one of the 2002 postseason games approached 43,000. In addition to watching from inside the park, fans can view the action for free from ground level through the brick arches in the right field wall on the port-walk.

From both a player's and spectator's perspective, this is unquestionably a much more comfortable park than Candlestick Park. It does get rather windy and chilly in the evenings, at times, but it is not nearly as bad as Candlestick Park. Being close to downtown San Francisco makes it an attractive after-work entertainment option, as well.

Although built expressly as a baseball park (unlike its predecessor Candlestick Park), Pacific Bell Park was used for football games when the San Francisco Demons XFL team played their home games there in the Spring 2001 season -- the XFL's only season. In addition, the collegiate ranks also played at the park twice yearly, with the San

Francisco Bowl and East-West Shrine Classic games. To accommodate football, groundskeepers set up temporary bleachers that stretch from left center field to the right field bullpen area.

On January 1, 2004, the park became officially known as "SBC Park." Pacific Bell had undergone a merger with Southwestern Bell Corporation some years earlier. The company wanted to advance the name recognition of the new corporation and thus exercised its right to change the name. On March 1, 2006, the park was officially renamed again to "AT&T Park." The new name reflected SBC's adoption of the AT&T brand following its acquisition in 2005. The new AT&T created America's largest telecommunications company.

Chapter 14: San Francisco Giants All-time Teams

All-Time 50th Anniversary Franchise Player (1958 - 2007)

WILLIE MAYS

All-Time 50th Anniversary Golden Dream Team (1958 - 2007)

Starting Players

1st Base: Willie McCovey
2nd Base: Jeff Kent
3rd Base: Matt Williams
Shortstop: Rich Aurilia
Catcher: Dick Dietz
Left Fielder: Barry Bonds
Center Fielder: Willie Mays
Right Fielder: Bobby Bonds
Utility / Bench: Orlando Cepeda
Right-Handed Starting Pitcher: Juan Marichal
Left-Handed Starting Pitcher: Vida Blue

Right-Handed Relief Pitcher: Rod Beck
Left-Handed Relief Pitcher: Gary Lavelle
Manager: Dusty Baker

Reserve Players

Right-Handed Starting Pitcher: Gaylord Perry
Right-Handed Starting Pitcher: Jack Sanford
Left-Handed Starting Pitcher: Mike McCormick
Right-Handed Relief Pitcher: Greg Minton
Right-Handed Relief Pitcher: Robb Nen
Reserve Catcher: Tom Haller
Reserve 1st Base: Will Clark
Reserve 2nd Base: Robby Thompson
Reserve Shortstop: Chris Speier
Reserve Outfielder: Jack Clark
Reserve Outfielder: Kevin Mitchell
Reserve Manager: Roger Craig
Selected by Chuck Nan in mid-2006

All-Time Candlestick Park Era Team (1960 - 1999)

1st Base: Willie McCovey
2nd Base: Robby Thompson
3rd Base: Matt Williams
Shortstop: Chris Speier
Catcher: Tom Haller
Left Fielder: Barry Bonds
Center Fielder: Willie Mays
Right Fielder: Bobby Bonds
Utility: Orlando Cepeda
Right-Handed Starting Pitcher: Juan Marichal
Left-Handed Starting Pitcher: Mike McCormick
Relief Pitcher: Rod Beck
Manager: Dusty Baker
Selected by fan vote in 1999

All-Time 25th Anniversary (Silver) Team (25 Giant Years)

1st Base: Willie McCovey
2nd Base: Tito Fuentes
3rd Base: Jim Davenport
Shortstop: Johnnie LeMaster
Catcher: Tom Haller
Left Fielder: Gary Matthews
Center Fielder: Willie Mays
Right Fielder: Jack Clark
Utility: Orlando Cepeda
Right-Handed Starting Pitcher: Juan Marichal
Left-Handed Starting Pitcher: Vida Blue
Right-Handed Relief Pitcher: Stu Miller
Left-Handed Relief Pitcher: Al Holland
Manager: Frank Robinson
Selected by fan vote at conclusion of 1981 season for 1982

ALL-DECADE TEAMS

1960s

1st Base: Willie McCovey
2nd Base: Tito Fuentes
3rd Base: Jim Davenport
Shortstop: Jose Pagan
Catcher: Tom Haller
Outfielder: Orlando Cepeda
Outfielder: Willie Mays
Outfielder: Felipe Alou
Right-Handed Starting Pitcher: Juan Marichal
Left-Handed Starting Pitcher: Mike McCormick
Relief Pitcher: Stu Miller
Selected by Bay Area media in 1999

1970s

1st Base: Willie McCovey
2nd Base: Tito Fuentes
3rd Base: Darrell Evans
Shortstop: Chris Speier
Catcher: Mike Sadek
Outfielder: Jack Clark
Outfielder: Willie Mays
Outfielder: Bobby Bonds
Right-Handed Starting Pitcher: Juan Marichal
Left-Handed Starting Pitcher: Vida Blue
Relief Pitcher: Gary Lavelle
Selected by Bay Area media in 1999

1980s

1st Base: Will Clark
2nd Base: Robby Thompson
3rd Base: Matt Williams
Shortstop: Jose Uribe
Catcher: Bob Brenly
Outfielder: Kevin Mitchell
Outfielder: Jeff Leonard
Outfielder: Chili Davis
Right-Handed Starting Pitcher: Mike Krukow
Left-Handed Starting Pitcher: Dave Dravecky
Relief Pitcher: Greg Minton
Selected by Bay Area media in 1999

1990s

1st Base: Will Clark
2nd Base: Jeff Kent
3rd Base: Matt Williams
Shortstop: Royce Clayton
Catcher: Kirt Manwaring
Outfielder: Barry Bonds

Outfielder: Darren Lewis
Outfielder: Willie McGee
Right-Handed Starting Pitcher: John Burkett
Left-Handed Starting Pitcher: Shawn Estes
Relief Pitcher: Rod Beck
Selected by Bay Area media in 1999

2000s

1st Base: J.T. Snow
2nd Base: Jeff Kent
3rd Base: Pedro Feliz
Shortstop: Rich Aurilia / Omar Vizquel (Tie)
Catcher: Mike Matheny
Outfielder: Barry Bonds
Outfielder: Moises Alou
Outfielder: Randy Winn
Right-Handed Starting Pitcher: Jason Schmidt
Left-Handed Starting Pitcher: Noah Lowry
Relief Pitcher: Robb Nen
Selected by Chuck Nan in mid-2006

Chapter 15: Epilogue

In the literary world, one accepted definition for an epilogue is "a short addition or concluding section at the end of a literary work, often dealing with the future of its characters, also called an afterword." Still another definition is "a piece of writing at the end of a work of drama, usually used to bring closure to the work." At this crossroad, I seek not to provide an ending or closure, but rather a brief pit stop to segway into the future. I will try my best to be non-cliché here, though.

While certainly possessing drama, and with characters, these experiences throughout the years have truly spanned all of the literary genres. Besides being filled with drama, it has also contained humor, documentary, legend and fiction, among others. It is one continous diary with many, many scenes, screening daily. With the flow of players, successes, defeats, happiness, joys, frustrations, etc., we have witnessed life, real life.

The Giants have had a significant impact on the city of San Franciso, the greater Bay Area, northern California and the game of baseball. They have made an impact on the lives of countless fans, both casual and hardcore and all varying degrees between. Many of us have invested a large amount of personal time, emotion, energy, enthusiasm and money over the years. The point is, the team has become woven into the fabric of our sports, entertainment and social lives; it is a relationship.

Sadly, the one most difficult void to cope with is the absence, the emptiness and disappointment of not experiencing, even once, a World Series champsionship. I do not like broaching this subject, because I do not want it to overshadow anything, however it has to be mentioned. This fact does not, nor should it ever, diminish the efforts we have witnessed and the beauty we have experienced. Anything less than triumphant accolades would be a gross injustice to the franchise, players, management and fans.

We as fans play different roles. We are critics. We are amatuer general managers. We are field managers. We are scouts. For me, I have learned to enjoy the game best when I sit back and appreciate the art and movment, the strategy. The beauty of baseball is the pitch-by-pitch intriege, the sights, sounds and smells. But most of all the beauty is the indellible memories that last forever.

One realization that I have learned from watching baseball is that you can never give up. This sounds cliché, but it is the truth. This is in spite of what the score is, what inning it is or what long odds you may feel are staring at you. There is always hope and the possibility of making that miracolous comeback. Optimism is the best ideal that any fan can have. It is an ideal that all true fans, of any sport or team, should have. Truth is stranger than fiction, they say. Entire momentum swings can occur on any pitch. A team is never out of it, even if down to their last strike.

Author Profile

Chuck Nan is a sports journalist and broadcaster in the Bay Area. Nan received his Bachelor's Degree in Finance from Loyola Marymount University in Los Angeles. For many years, he worked in the financial services industry, holding positions in operations, customer service and project management.

After a successful business career, Nan started his own firm, SportsQuest Tours that specialized in fan travel to sporting events worldwide. He also served as Media Relations Director, and co-hosted several popular shows, for a local all-sports format radio station, covering all of the local professional and college teams and many high profile sports events.

Chuck has recently turned to the written form of sports journalism. He is the Sports Editor for his hometown paper the *Martinez News-Gazette*. His first formally published piece was entitled "San Francisco Giants Spring Tour of Japan, March 1970" in *Elysian Fields Quarterly-The Baseball Review* in summer, 2004. Chuck has also had smaller articles published by SABR (Society for American Baseball Research) in their annual releases, *The Baseball Research Journal* and *The National Pastime*.

Nan is also involved with youth baseball as a coach, instructor and administrator. In the past years, Chuck has worked with the San Francisco Giants Youth Baseball Summer Camp and EJ Sports, run by former Giants' players, Rob Andrews and Erik Johnson, respectively and BayArea Baseball of Hayward. He has also worked with the baseball program at Alhambra High School in Martinez.

A true native of San Francisco, Chuck grew up just 10 minutes from Candlestick Park. The Giants were his first sports love at age six, and still are. He has been a season ticket holder for many years and seen several hundred games in his life. Chuck has spent many a frigid summer night at the 'Stick watching his beloved team.

Nan resides with his family in Martinez, California.

Printed in the United States
97193LV00004B/19/A